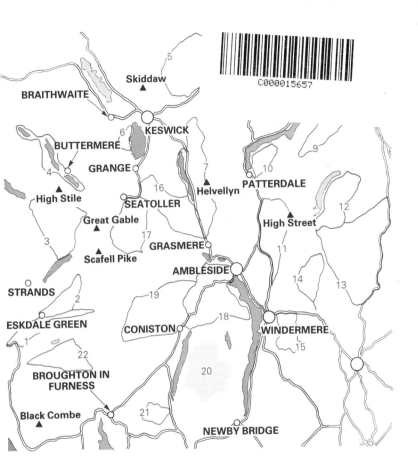

1. Eskdale and Ravenglass
2. Burnmoor Tarn and Miterdale
3. Wasdale and Ennerdale
4. Buttermere, Crummock Water and Loweswater
5. Tour of Blencathra
6. Tour of Cat Bells
7. The Helvellyn Range Complete
8. Moor Divock
9. Loadpot Hill
10. Tour of Place Fell
11. High Street South
12. Haweswater and Swindale
13. Longsleddale and Wet Sleddale
14. Tour of Kentmere
15. Windermere and Crook
16. Greenup Edge and Blea Tarn
17. Esk Hause and Stake Pass
18. Loughrigg Terrace, Tilberthwaite and Claife Heights
19. Walna Scar Road and Wrynose Pass
20. Grizedale Forest
21. Subberthwaite Common
22. Devoke Water and Ulpha Fell

Published by the Ernest Press 1991
© Copyright Jeremy Ashcroft

British Library Cataloguing-in-Publication Data
Ashcroft Jeremy, 1959-
More routes in the Lakes, Howgills & Yorkshire Dales –
(Mountain Bike Guide)
I. Title   II. Series
796.609427

ISBN 0 948153 13 X

Typeset by EMS Phototypesetting, Berwick
Origination by Par Graphics
Printed by Martin's of Berwick
Bound by Hunter & Foulis

MOUNTAIN BIKE GUIDE

More routes in the Lakes, Howgills & the Yorkshire Dales

by

JEREMY ASHCROFT

Contents

ROUTES – Lake District

ROUTES – Howgills and the Yorkshire Dales

Acknowledgements

The preparation of this guide book would have been impossible without the unstinting assistance of many people – I am grateful to them all. Loraine for checking the MS and accompanying me on routes; Chris Betts, for his photographs and for accompanying me on routes; Geoff Langman, Barbara Russell and James Bradshaw, for accompanying me on routes. I would also like to thank Jim Iddon for the loan of his computer and Phil McIver of Grange Cycles for technical assistance.

The publishers wish to acknowledge editorial assistance and supervision of production from Susan Hodgkiss.

Jeremy Ashcroft
Mewith, September 1991

Jeremy Ashcroft was born in Liverpool in 1959. He studied Technical Illustration at Blackpool College of Art. He works as a freelance illustrator and author. Jeremy has been climbing regularly, at home and abroad, since 1975 and was a member of his local Mountain Rescue Team for 6 years. He has been mountain biking since 1984. He lives with his wife in Mewith on the southern border of the Dales.

INTRODUCTION

The huge success of the 'Mountain Bike Guide: The Lake District, The Howgills & The Yorkshire Dales' determined the demand for a further companion guide offering more routes within the boundaries of the Lake District National Park and the Yorkshire Dales National Park. These areas offer, without doubt, the greatest potential for mountain biking in this country. There are literally hundreds of miles of 'Rights of Way' open to cyclists across summits, passes, moorland and along valleys. The range of challenges is tremendous. This companion guide details easy routes which offer peace and tranquillity amongst fine scenery with few technical or navigational problems. There are also the full-blown 'Mountain' bike rides which will test even the most experienced and accomplished riders.

The aim of this guide book is to select and detail the best routes available from the two national parks. Each route meets simple basic criteria: it should be a circular tour and at least ⅔ of the total distance should be rideable; it should also be possible to complete the route within a day. In addition each route is described in the direction which gives the shortest ascent and the longest downhill run. To fully enjoy mountain biking amongst 'real' mountains it is important that you accept a certain amount of pushing or carrying. If you limit yourself solely to routes that can be ridden throughout their entirety, then you will close the door on most of the routes in this book and a lot of wonderful experiences.

Like any other activity in the mountains, mountain biking is potentially dangerous. On undertaking any excursion into the mountains you should consider, as far as possible, the level of risk you are prepared to expose yourself to, and if anything went wrong what the consequences would be to yourself and to other people. The sudden changes in weather, precipitous terrain and remoteness from help are all key elements which must be taken seriously. Only attempt routes that you know are within your personal limits – there is nothing more rewarding than returning from a hard day in the hills and knowing at the back of your mind that you still had plenty in reserve.

ENVIRONMENT

Both the Lake District and Yorkshire Dales National Parks are highly sensitive mountain areas that must be treated with the greatest respect if they are to remain unspoilt. Over the last few decades there has been a tremendous increase in the number of people using these areas for recreational purposes, which in some parts of the parks could be seen to have reached saturation point. Apart from the effect which tourism has made upon the area, there is the extensive damage caused by agriculture and industry. Any relatively new activity like mountain biking will be used as a scape-goat for any environmental damage by other groups with a vested interest.

It is our love for mountains, moors and hills that draws us, as mountain bikers, back time and time again; we seek to enjoy them not destroy them – we know this but others do not. Each individual mountain biker should regard himself as an ambassador of the sport. Your behaviour to the environment and to others in the environment should be impeccable. You should do all in your power to avoid damage by yourself and others. Simple actions can make all the difference:

Never ride across ground that can be permanently eroded (i.e. bogs, scree etc.) get off and walk or better still find a way round.

Never skid and avoid locking your wheels when braking.

Set your bike up so that it is equipped sympathetically (e.g. wide tyres for greater surface contact area, resin pedals that deform themselves rather than scratch rocks etc.)

Do not travel in large groups, 5-6 should be regarded as the maximum.

Two codes have been established which are particularly relevant to mountain biking.

The Off-Road Code

Issued by the Mountain Bike Club.
Only ride where you know you have a legal right.
Always yield to horses and pedestrians.
Avoid animals and crops. In some circumstances this may not be possible, at which times contact should be kept to a minimum.
Take all litter with you.
Leave all gates as found.
Keep the noise down.
Don't get annoyed with anyone, it never solves any problems.
Always try to be self-sufficient, for you and your bike.
Never create a fire hazard.

The Country Code

Issued by the Countryside Commission
Enjoy the countryside and respect its life and work.
Guard against all risk of fire.
Fasten all gates.
Keep your dogs under close control.
Keep to public paths across farmland.

Use gates and stiles to cross fences, hedges and walls.
Leave livestock, crops and machinery alone.
Take your litter home.
Help keep all water clean.
Protect wildlife, plants and trees.
Take special care on country roads.
Make no unnecessary noise.

RIGHTS OF WAY

Off-road cyclists have right of way on virtually all public bridleways and other tracks of higher status (e.g. BOAT – by-way open to all traffic and RUPP – road used as a public path). On bridleways cyclists must give way to walkers and horse riders and on all rights of way it is an offence to cycle recklessly, carelessly and under the influence of drink! There is no right of way for cyclists on public footpaths.

Although every care has been taken in the production and checking of this guide book there will inevitably be misinterpretations and information relating to the status of rights of way will change with passage of time. Therefore the representation in this guide book of any route is no evidence of the existence of right of way. If you are in any doubt you can check the Definitive Maps which are held by the appropriate County Council.

If you are asked by a landowner or occupier to leave the land or route you are on because you are thought to be trespassing, do so by the shortest practicable route, as quickly as you can. Do not seek confrontation, it will achieve nothing; if you believe you have right of way check with the local authorities and get them to pursue the matter – if you cause undue friction mountain biking will suffer.

Further information can be found in Cycling Off-Road and the Law issued by the Cyclists' Touring Club.

MAPS

This guide book is specifically designed to be used with a map and not by itself. Although there are numerous proprietery maps available the Ordnance Survey maps are the only real choice. They provide precise cartographic information and are constantly being updated.

At the beginning of each route the relevant Ordnance Survey 1:25 000 or 1:50 000 scale maps are listed. The Lake District is also covered by 1:63 360 (1 inch to 1 mile) scale map which, because of its limited detail, cannot be recommended for anything other than route planning. It is always a good idea to have the map folded to the right area in a map case or a clear plastic bag. Even in the best conditions there is often a breeze that will make reading the map and refolding it difficult.

To attempt to explain map reading and navigational skills in the space available in this publication would be impractical: those requiring further information should read either of the following books:

Rober B. Matkin, *Map Reading*, Dalesman Books.

Eric Langmuir, *Mountain Craft and Leadership*, The Scottish Sports Council.

EQUIPMENT

The Bike

The type of mountain bike you use is of course a highly personal thing but if you are going to take it into 'real' mountain bike country it should be as light as possible, mechanically sound with effective brakes and uncluttered. Mud guards, racks and bottle cages are OK on the road but are a waste of time in the hills – adding to weight and susceptible to damage, they cause no end of problems. Tyres with at least a 2 ins. section should be fitted as they have a large contact surface area, minimising any damage to soft ground. At some point on all the routes you are likely to have to carry your bike so it is essential that you pad the frame accordingly. Closed-cell foam is about the best, it is waterproof, cheap, comfortable and keeps its shape well – you cannot really overdo the padding particularly if you are attempting a route that involves sustained carrying.

Carry a basic tool kit and spares so that you can make adjustments and repairs but don't go over the top – remember you have to carry all your equipment.

The Biker

Navigation and Survival.

Regardless of whatever else you take with you, the following items should be regarded as essential and you should be fully familiar with their use:

Map – relevant to the area!

Compass.

Survival Bag (8ft × 4ft 500 gauge polythene bag).

Helmet

Whistle – International Alpine Distress Signal – six blasts followed by a pause of a minute then a repetition.

Torch – International Alpine Distress Signal – six flashes followed by a pause of a minute then a repetition of the six flashes.

Emergency rations.

Clothing

Normal cycling clothing is worse than useless for the range of conditions that you will encounter amongst this country's hills and mountains. Skin tops and shorts simply do not offer the level of protection to keep you warm and dry, and touring shoes do not give enough grip or support. In selecting clothing it is better to choose from the large range designed for climbers and walkers. A layer system is the best approach as this will allow you to strip or dress according to the conditions or whether you are moving or at rest. Essentially the combination of clothes you choose should be windproof, waterproof and insulate even when wet. Use a rucksack or bum bag to carry clothes and equipment so that if you become separated from your bike your hands are free from carrying panniers, saddle bags etc.

Conditions will also dictate footwear but generally it should have good grip (Vibram or Skywalker type soles are about the best) and should support both the foot and the ankle. If you decide to wear training shoes (not recommended particularly for beginners) you should use the type designed for fell runners – some compounds used in the soles of training shoes are lethal on wet grass and rock.

ACCIDENT PROCEDURE

Do any immediate First Aid that is necessary. Stop any bleeding by applying clean dressings and bandaging firmly. If the patient is unconscious, make sure that he is not choking with his tongue blocking the back of his throat.

Make the patient as comfortable as possible and treat for shock. Keep him warm, putting spare clothing etc as insulation underneath him. Warm sweet drinks should be given to those who are conscious and suffering from exhaustion or exposure. Never give drinks to anyone with chest, abdominal or head injuries, or any injured patient who may be transported to hospital quickly and put under an anaesthetic. If a long carry of many hours is expected, then warm sugary drinks may be a life saver in case of shock and when no morphia is available. (For further advice see the section on First Aid).

Give the International Alpine Distress Signal – six blasts on a whistle (or six shouts or flashes of a torch) followed by a pause of a minute then a repetition of the six blasts, shouts or whistles. Keep giving this signal system. If your signals are eventually heard you should hear an answering whistle – three blasts followed by a pause of a minute, repeated several times. If by chance your whistle or torch is missing and your voice doesn't carry because of the wind, you can wave a white or coloured cloth.

If your signal does not produce assistance, one or two (if possible) of the party must go down and contact the Police or the nearest Mountain Rescue Post. You should already be familiar with these; they may be marked on maps, though locations sometimes change and should be checked. The messenger must carry and give the following information concerning the accident.

Exact position, giving six-figure grid reference or, if this is not feasible, as much information as possible to enable a rescue party to go straight to the injured person.

Time of the accident.

How many people are injured.

Nature of the injuries.

If the injured person has to be left alone whilst you fetch help, first give him all your spare clothing to keep him warm. If his injuries permit, move him to a good sheltered position, otherwise erect a wind-break around him. It may be many hours before a rescue party reaches him, the weather may worsen and he may easily die of shock and exposure in the meantime unless you take very careful precautions.

If he is conscious, reassure him, leave him a torch and whistle to guide the rescue party to his aid. If unconscious, belay him to a rock if possible to prevent him from falling further or from wandering off in a dazed condition if he gains consciousness. It is wise to leave a cheering message before you leave him in case he should regain consciousness. If possible mark the position of the patient with a bright piece of clothing or equipment. A cairn of stones will be better than no position mark at all.

When you have done everything possible for the patient go and fetch help, descending quickly but carefully.

First Aid

Every party on the hills should carry a first aid pack. This should contain as a minimum:

Plasters (for blisters and cuts); lint or gauze (for dressings, etc); Acriflavine cream (antiseptic and soothing cream useful for burns, cuts, etc); and a selection of bandages.

Salt is a very useful commodity in mountains and may sometimes relieve cramp. A solution of salt makes a good dressing for cuts, burns and sprains.

Treatment

Medical treatment is obviously best left in the hands of a doctor or someone highly skilled in first aid but, if an accident does occur, it may be necessary for an unskilled person to give immediate first aid before a rescue party can be summoned. Every mountain biker should therefore learn at least the rudiments of First Aid, and this can be done through the St. John Ambulance Association, the British Red Cross Society or, in Scotland, the St. Andrew's Ambulance Association.

The notes below are intended purely as a simple guide for laymen faced with a mountain accident.

General Principles
Check the airway. Check it frequently and keep it clear.
Stop any bleeding and apply dressing to open wounds.
Do not move the patient unless you are quite sure that there is no injury to the spine.
Treat for shock. Keep warm and relieve pain.
Immobilize broken limbs to relieve pain and prevent any further damage.
Do not experiment. When in doubt, do as little First Aid as possible since an unskilled person can do considerable damage by applying the wrong treatment.

Shock
Shock is present in almost all cases of accident. The symptoms are pallor, weak and rapid pulse, cold, clammy skin, and hunger for air. Make the patient comfortable and insulate him from the cold ground. Reassure him, allay anxiety and relieve pain. Never overheat a shocked patient.

Burns and Scalds
Use a dry sterile dressing on a wound and treat the patient for pain and shock. Leave any adhering clothing on a burn. Remove hot wet clothing from a scald.

Cuts and Wounds
Cut away clothing to make sure there is no dangerous bleeding if it is suspected. Stop any bleeding by applying direct pressure on the wound with a clean dressing or pad and then a bandage.

Sprained, Twisted and Dislocated Ankles
In general, do not remove boot – it forms an excellent splint and sufficient relief from swelling can usually be obtained by loosening the laces. If boot is removed apply cold compress and bandage firmly to limit swelling.

Cramp
Massage the affected part and apply warmth. It may sometimes be relieved by drinking a salt solution or eating a few grains.

Frostbite
Early or superficial frostbite is best treated by applying body warmth or breathing on the cold parts until sensation returns. The warm skin of the crutch or the armpit is good or if possible immersing the part in warm water. Once a frostbitten part has been rewarmed, keep it warm. Do not rub. Treatment of deep or established frostbite should be delayed until hospital treatment can be given. Protect the parts from rubbing or banging for the tissue is devitalised and will readily tear.

Snakebite

The only poisonous snake in Britain is the adder, but it is a frequenter of hill districts.

The commonest symptoms are fright and fear of death. Reassurance is vital. Death from snake bite is extremely rare.

Keep the patient at rest.

Immobilize the bitten part as for a fracture and apply a firm bandage on the heart side of the bite.

Administer analgesia (e.g. asprin) but no morphia.

Fractures

Fractures must be immobilized before the patient is carried down on a stretcher, but if you have no experience or training in First Aid, it is probably better not to try to immobilize a fracture before the Rescue Party arrives, unless it is causing the patient extreme pain. Do not try to straighten a broken limb.

Arm. Bandage the upper arm to the chest (if splints are available, first bandage these to the arm), and either put the forearm in a sling or bandage it also to the chest, whichever is more comfortable for the patient.

Leg. Bandage the injured leg to the sound one at the ankles, knees and hips, padding well between the knees, or bandage the leg to a splint if available. Avoid moving the injured leg and do not try to straighten.

Collar Bone. Place the hand near the other collar bone and bandage the whole shoulder and arm to the chest.

Spine. On no account move the patient. A spinal injury is often difficult to diagnose, but signs are pain in the back or numbness in the legs. If in the slightest doubt, treat as a spinal injury, and do not move until you have plenty of helpers and a proper stretcher.

Neck. Carefully lay the patient flat on his back. Place a pair of boots, one on each side of the head, with the soles facing outwards and the uppers crossing under the nape of the neck. Narrow triangular bandages can then be tied firmly round the boots and head across the forehead and chin.

Jaw. Support the jaw with the hand, then bandage. Don't allow the patient to lie back or he will choke as he cannot swallow.

Head Injuries

Check the airway frequently and keep it clear. Stop any bleeding by applying a sterile pad and bandage firmly, then place the patient in the recovery position.

Unconscious Patient

Do not administer drinks or morphia. Make sure breathing is unobstructed and remove any dentures. Turn the patient on his side in the coma position to prevent the tongue falling back and obstructing the airway and to help the drainage of secretions.

Heat Exhaustion

Reduce temperature by moving into cool shade, using cold water and/or helping respiration by increasing air movement – fanning. Apply preventive action – i.e. the giving of salt in solution.

Exposure

Exposure is caused by exhaustion and severe chilling of the body surface, usually in windy and wet conditions. This is one of the most common reasons for rescue calls in mountains and must be guarded against continually. Additional information can be found in Mountain Hypothermia, issued by the British Mountaineering Council.

Signs and Symptoms:

Complaints of cold, tiredness, cramp.
Mental and physical lethargy. Lack of understanding of simple questions and directions.
Slurring speech.
Irrational or violent behaviour.
Abnormality of vision.
Collapse and coma.
These may not all be present nor in the order given.

All cases should be treated immediately, for mild cases can rapidly become very serious. Suspect others, and yourself, of being mild cases and protect the party from being reduced to the same condition.

Prevention:

Wear good clothing including windproof and waterproof garments.
Avoid getting over-tired.
Do not go too long without energy-giving foods.
If any member of a party is becoming tired, cold and wet, the group should go down into a more sheltered area.

Treatment:

Stop. Provide shelter from the elements causing exposure. Having found a spot, put up a tent or use the emergency bivouac provided by rucksack and 8ft × 4ft 500 gauge polythene bag. Give the patient prolonged rest.

Immediately insulate the patient from further heat loss. Insulation from the cold ground is particularly important. Cover for head, face and neck is a great help.

Place the patient in a horizontal position and if possible place a warm companion alongside him.

Anxiety and mental stress is often an important contributory factor. Be cheerful and encouraging.

If there is no breathing in severe cases, mouth to mouth resuscitation should be given until normal breathing is obtained.

Do not rub the patient to restore circulation.

Do not allow further exertion and thereby use up essential energy.

Do not give alcohol.

If in doubt send for help but prompt action, good equipment and good leadership will provide the important safeguards against exposure.

The sections on Accident Procedure and First Aid were reproduced with the kind permission of the British Mountaineering Council from their excellent booklet 'Safety on Mountains'.

THE ROUTES

Generally the routes fit into three main categories – valley routes, those that cross passes, and those that visit summits. When selecting a route you should carefully balance your experience and fitness against its grade, distance and height gain. Only attempt routes that are within your personal limits. Rapid weather changes, navigational errors, accidents and mechanical problems are all the more difficult to deal with if you have pushed yourself too much and attempted a route beyond your capability.

Times

The times given for each route are based on a fit competent party with the benefit of good conditions. Lack of experience and poor conditions can greatly extend the time needed to complete a route; this should be taken into account before commencing – particularly in winter when the daylight hours are short.

Grades

Each route has been graded according to its technical difficulty. Adjectives have been used to describe how an experienced mountain biker new to the district would assess the levels of difficulty encountered.

Easy – no significant difficulties
Moderate – mostly good going but with some difficulties
Difficult – more sustained difficulties
Very Difficult – routes across the harder passes and that reach easier summits
Severe – routes that reach summits and cross very dangerous terrain
Very Severe – the limit of feasible mountain biking at this time!

The grades selected for each route have been agreed only by the limited number of people involved in the production of this guide book. Until a grading system has been firmly established and recognized by a broad spectrum of mountain bikers, the grades listed can be nothing more than subjective.

Abbreviations

E	East
ft	Feet
L	Left (used in relation to the direction of travel)
m	Miles
N	North
NE	North East
NW	North West
O.S.	Ordnance Survey
R	Right (used in relation to the direction of travel)
S	South
SE	South East
SW	South West
W	West
yds	Yards
°	Degrees from north

Illustrations

Each route is illustrated by either a map or a relief map and a photograph. Generally a straightforward map is used to show the course of a route, but where steep complicated terrain dictates, a relief map has been used instead. There is no consistency in scale as it was considered more important to show the whole route on either a single page or a two page spread – eliminating the need to turn pages to see the whole route. The photographs are to highlight interesting features and to give an idea of the character of particular routes.

ESKDALE AND RAVENGLASS

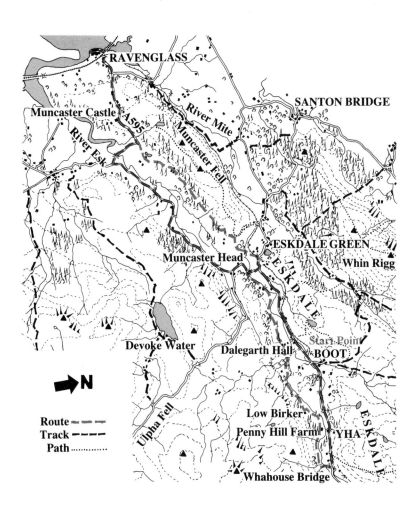

Eskdale and Ravenglass

Grade: Easy
Time: 4½ Hours
Height Gain: 836ft
Distance: 20 Miles – 8 off road, 12 on road
Terrain: Wooded valley and coast
Surface: Grassy bridleway, farm track and road
Start Point Grid Reference: 174007, Dalegarth Station
Maps: O.S. The English Lakes 1:25 000 SW sheet

Three main routes follow the River Esk along Eskdale to its mouth at Ravenglass. These are a road, a narrow gauge railway (Ravenglass to Eskdale Railway) and, of most interest to mountain bikers, a bridleway. The bridleway starts at Whahouse Bridge just below Hardknott Pass and gives eight miles of easy off road riding through pleasant woodland and along good farm tracks.

This route is ideal for beginners and family groups as it provides no real navigational problems and makes only negligible height gains. There are numerous access points from the bridleway to the valley road allowing the route to be shortened.

Route Description

From Dalegarth Station follow the valley road E for 2m to Whahouse Bridge. Cross the bridge and join the bridleway on the other side. Follow the bridleway S alongside the River Esk then up through the woods to a T junction. Turn R and head W along the bridleway through Penny Hill Farm to Doctor Bridge on the river. Do not cross the bridge – instead turn L and follow the bridleway as it heads SW to a junction at Low Birker. At the junction turn R and follow the bridleway W for just over 1m to a ford and foot bridge. Cross the ford and continue heading W along the bridleway. After 1¼m the bridleway swings SW alongside the river and joins the valley road at Forge Bridge.

From Forge Bridge take the valley road N then W to Eskdale Green Station. Do not cross the bridge over the railway – instead take the bridleway at the back of the station buildings and follow it SW along the lane, across the ford then up through woodland. Once out of the trees the bridleway swings W across pasture to join a track after 300yds. Turn L onto the track and follow it S to the farm at Muncaster Head. Pass the farm and turn R onto another track. Follow the track

19

as it heads generally SW for 1½m to a fork just after High Eskholme. At the fork take the L branch and follow the bridleway S then SW alongside a plantation. Once past the trees the bridleway swings S again then finally W to join the A595. Turn R onto the A595 and follow it N then W for 1½m to the Ravenglass turning. At the junction turn L and follow the road into Ravenglass.

The return leg is all by road. From Ravenglass back-track to the A595 which is then followed E then S for 2m to the Eskdale turning – 300 yds after crossing the River Esk at Muncaster Bridge. At the junction turn L and follow the road for 3m as it winds its way NE to a T junction. At the junction turn L and follow the road N to another junction at the King George IV pub. Turn R onto the Eskdale valley road and follow it E for 1¾m back to Dalegarth Station.

Ford in Bank Wood, Eskdale Green

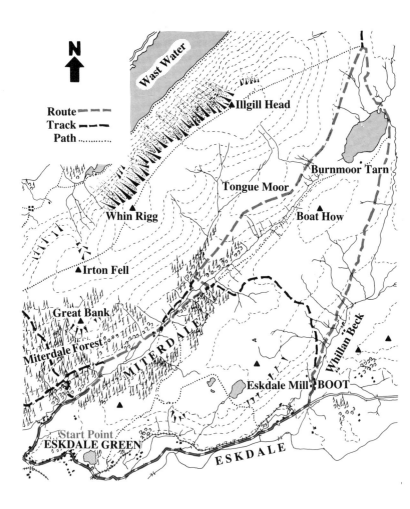

N

Route -- --
Track -- --
Path ....

Wast Water

Illgill Head

Burnmoor Tarn

Tongue Moor

Whin Rigg

Boat How

Irton Fell

Great Bank

Miterdale Forest

MITERDALE

Whillan Beck

Eskdale Mill   BOOT

Start Point
ESKDALE GREEN

ESKDALE

Burnmoor Tarn and Miterdale

Grade: Difficult
Time: 2½-3 Hours
Height Gain: 955ft
Distance: 11 Miles – 7 off road, 4 on road
Terrain: Valleys and mountain pass
Surface: Generally well-graded tracks with some boggy and some rocky sections
Start Point Grid Reference: 142001, Eskdale Green
Maps: O.S. The English Lakes 1:25 000 SW sheet

The western slopes of Scafell run off into a depression occupied by Burnmoor Tarn. They then rise again to form a horseshoe of fells between Eskdale and Wasdale. Lying at the centre of these fells is the secluded valley of Miterdale.

A bridleway links Wasdale with Eskdale via Burnmoor Tarn. Originally this route was a 'Corpse Road' used to transport the dead of Wasdale for burial at the church at Boot. Connecting with this bridleway is another from Miterdale – the two routes meet half a mile to the north of Burnmoor Tarn.

A circuit of these two bridleways gives a surprisingly challenging mountain bike tour. The pleasant pastoral landscape found in Eskdale and Miterdale gives very easy riding and belies the harder stuff to be had on the desolate, open moorland around Burnmoor Tarn.

Route Description

From Eskdale Green take the valley road and follow it as it winds E for just over ½m to a junction (opposite the King George IV pub). At the junction turn L and follow the road E for 2m to a turning for Boot. Turn L and follow the lane through Boot and cross the bridge at Eskdale Mill. On the other side of the bridge join a track and follow it a short distance as it zigzags to a fork. Take the R branch. This is the start of the bridleway to Burnmoor Tarn (Coffin Road). It climbs steeply at first, then gradually eases and heads NE for 2m to a low col overlooking Burnmoor Tarn. The bridleway now descends N then NW for 1¼m skirting Burnmoor Tarn and finally climbing to another low col.

This col is the highest point reached by the 'Coffin Road' and is something of a cross-roads. The 'Coffin Road' itself continues N and descends into Wasdale;

Porterthwaite Bridge, Miterdale

to the W a path climbs the steep fell side to Illgill Head and to the SW the Miterdale bridleway climbs steadily towards Tongue Moor. Take the Miterdale bridleway and follow it SW across boggy moorland – vague at first. After 1m the bridleway levels, continue SW as it traverses above the crags on Tongue Moor. Once the crags are passed the bridleway gives an exhilarating descent to Miterdale Head. From Miterdale Head cross the River Mite and follow the bridleway on the SE bank of the river for $^{3}/_{4}$m re-crossing it to Low Place. At Low Place join the access track and follow it SW then S on the valley road to the main bridge over the River Mite. Cross the bridge and follow the valley road SW for 1m to a T junction. Turn L and follow the road back to Eskdale Green.

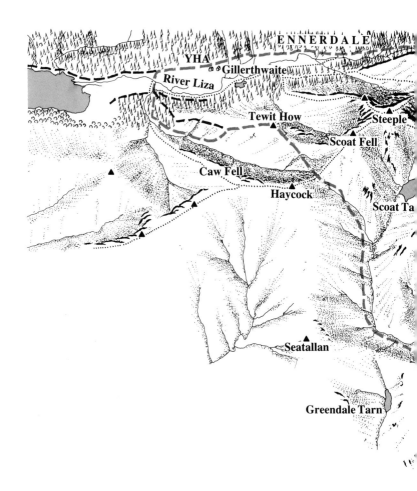

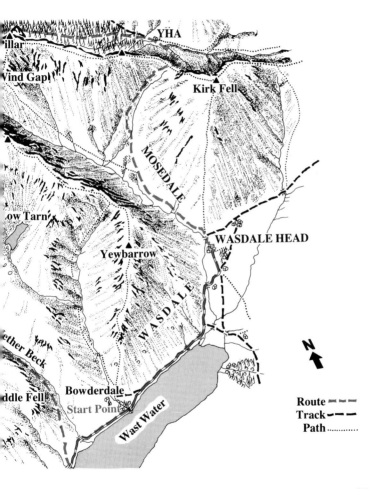

illar

YHA

ind Gap!

Kirk Fell

MOSEDALE

ow Tarn

WASDALE HEAD

Yewbarrow

WASDALE

ether Beck

ddle Fell

Bowderdale

Start Point

Wast Water

N

Route ---
Track ---
Path ....

Wasdale and Ennerdale

Grade: Severe
Time: 5 Hours
Height Gain: 3179ft
Distance: 15 Miles – 12½ off road, 2½ on road
Terrain: High mountain passes
Surface: Steep, rocky mountain tracks, exposed ridge, forestry roads, well-graded pack-horse track and valley road
Start Point Grid Reference: 168068, Overbeck Bridge, Wast Water SW sheet
Maps: O.S. The English Lake District 1:25 000 SW and NW sheets

Separating Wasdale and Ennerdale is a range of high rugged mountains centered around Pillar and Steeple. There are no roads directly linking the two valleys. Only at Calder Bridge, ten miles to the west does the terrain relent enough to allow passage of a narrow fell road. For mountain bikers, however, there are two other crossings: the popular route over Black Sail Pass, a well-graded packhorse route that gives a superb descent on the Wasdale side; and the rough, little frequented pass at the col between Haycock and Scoat Fell. The latter gives particularly challenging mountain biking – the ascent from Wasdale demands a considerable amount of carrying.

This route passes through some particularly fine mountain scenery. Both the Wasdale and Ennerdale sides have deeply recessed corries, with steep head walls and fast flowing becks. The crowning glory though is Pillar Rock, which lies on the north face of Pillar and is separated by a steep rocky defile known as Jordan Gap. The crossing of Jordan Gap requires rock climbing skills which gives it the unique claim to fame as the only peak in Lakeland which cannot be reached by walkers.

Route Description

From the carpark at Overbeck Bridge, head SW along the Wast Water road for ¾m crossing Netherbeck Bridge to the start of a bridleway (sign). Turn R onto the bridleway, which is vague at first, and follow it up across rough fell side. The bridleway heads N and soon levels to join Nether Beck after ½m. Continue on the bridleway as it climbs alongside the L bank of Nether Beck, heading NW then N for 2m to a confluence of becks below Little Lad Crag. The bridleway then swings back to the NW and is followed up a steep pull into a shallow corrie. Continue NW through the corrie and climb its grassy back wall to gain the col between Haycock and Scoat Fell (NW sheet).

The col holds a commanding position overlooking Ennerdale Water. From the col, descend N over steep grass and traverse the head of Great Cove to Tewit How which is reached after ¾m. Tewit How affords expansive views of Ennerdale and is the start of the descent proper. Descend NW along the vague bridleway (small cairns) dropping down towards Ennerdale Forest and Woundell Beck – the last section down to the beck is very steep. The bridleway skirts the top side of the forest and is very overgrown – better to take advantage of the good forest track which starts at a gate by Woundell Beck. Follow the track N alongside the beck for ¾m to a junction. Turn L and head W to another junction. Turn R and follow the track NE to a bridge over the River Liza. Cross the bridge and turn R onto the main Ennerdale forest track. Follow the track E for 4m as it climbs easily to the YHA's Black Sail Hut.

The next section of the route is the crossing of Black Sail Pass. Continue along the track past the hut SE to a ford and bridge. Continue S as it skirts the forest edge (tree felling was going on when this route was checked). Follow the track as it climbs the steep fell side by Sail Beck and over an awkward rock step, at which point it leaves the beck and zigzags to the top of the pass. Again as you near the top of the pass the gradient eases and it is possible to ride. From Black Sail Pass there are spectacular views across Mosedale to Red Pike and Yewbarrow. You are now at the halfway point and the start of the best downhill run of the route. (Change from The English Lakes NW to The English Lakes SW O.S. map). The track drops SW then S into Mosedale over ideal mountain bike terrain and leads after 2m to Wasdale Head. Follow it easily at first from the pass over a short series of rock steps then down a fast stony section. The track then zigzags steeply down to a ford which crosses Gatherstone Beck, traverses the rough lower slopes of Kirk Fell and then opens out onto the valley floor. Keep an eye out to the SE for Scafell; it starts to come into view at this point. Continue easily down Mosedale, crossing a few entertaining fords to a junction with the track from Burnthwaite. Ignore the track to Burnthwaite and continue SW to the Wasdale Head Inn. At the inn join the Wast Water road and follow it SW back to Overbeck Bridge carpark.

BUTTERMERE, CRUMMOCK WATER AND LOWESWATER

Buttermere, Crummock Water and Loweswater

Grade: Moderate
Time: 4-4½ Hours
Height Gain: 1312ft
Distance: 16 Miles – 8½ off road, 7½ on road
Terrain: Exposed moorland, valleys and lake side
Surface: Valley roads, pleasant lake side tracks and boggy bridleways
Start Point Grid Reference: 176170, Buttermere
Maps: O.S. The English Lakes 1:25 000 NW sheet

Buttermere, Crummock Water and Loweswater form a trio of lakes which feed the River Cocker that flows along Lorton Vale to the Irish Sea. Buttermere and Crummock Water occupy the upper reaches of Lorton Vale and drain north-west, whilst Loweswater sits in a subsidiary valley and uniquely drains south-west into Crummock Water. This is unusual as all other lakes in the Lake District drain away from the central fells and not towards them, as with Loweswater.

Loweswater not only drains in the opposite direction but its setting is unusual as well. There is much more habitation and the surrounding fells are lower than those around Buttermere and Crummock Water, which seem to give it a much gentler atmosphere.

A series of bridleways link the south-western sides of the three lakes. When combined with the pleasant roads on the north-eastern sides, a fine mountain bike expedition can be had. Generally the riding is fairly easy, being mostly on well managed tracks. The exception to this is the link between Crummock Water and Loweswater which crosses a col on the south side of Mellbreak. If this section is missed out and the road taken instead, the route would only warrant an 'Easy' grade – and would be ideal for beginners.

Route Description

Take the B5289 SE from Buttermere village and follow it towards Honister Pass. After 2m a bridleway on the R at Gatesgarth is reached. Turn onto the bridleway and follow it SW past the farm and then across the valley floor at the head of Buttermere. Cross the bridge and then turn R onto the easy bridleway alongside Buttermere. Follow the bridleway NW for 1½m – the bridleway climbs slightly through Burtness Wood. The lower path is a permissive path and

31

not open to mountain bikes. Once past the end of Buttermere, continue NW alongside Buttermere Dubs – the beck that connects it to Crummock Water.

After 1½m Crummock Water is reached, and numerous paths climb W away from the lake. Ignore these paths and continue alongside the lake for another ½m. Follow the vague bridleway that swings W and leads to the sheepfolds alongside Scale Beck. Cross Scale Beck and pick up the still vague bridleway which starts to climb steeply W. Ascend the bridleway for ½m to a col that opens out onto the plateau at the head of Mosedale. A good track heads N down into Mosedale but this is classified as a path and not open to mountain bikers. The bridleway continues W across the boggy plateau – not at all clear on the ground. After 1m, a final pull leads to a more distinct bridleway. Back-track along this bridleway and follow it E then N down into Mosedale. After 1m the bridleway crosses Mosedale Beck and joins the good track from the col – a frustrating detour. Once joined, the track down Mosedale provides an excellent 1½m run N down into Loweswater village.

From Loweswater village turn L at the hotel and head NW to a T junction. Turn L again and follow the road W ¼m to the start of a bridleway on the L. Follow the bridleway W to a fork at Maggie's Bridge. Take the R fork and follow the pleasant bridleway NW for 1½m around Loweswater, through Holme Wood to the farm at Hudson Place. Pass through the farm and follow the lane N to the road at Waterend. Turn R onto the road and follow it SE then NE for 2½m back alongside Loweswater to Scalehill Bridge (over the River Cocker). Just up the hill (NE) from the bridge is the start of a bridleway (carpark). Turn R onto the bridleway and follow it as it climbs SE through Lanthwaite Wood – once in the woods the bridleway forks R after 300yds. After the junction the bridleway makes a short climb and swings E, clears the wood and leads along a lane to the B5289. Turn R onto the B5289 and follow it S then SE for 3m alongside Crummock Water and back to Buttermere.

Alternative Route (Easy)

Follow the normal route to the end of Buttermere, but instead of heading for Crummock Water, cross Buttermere Dub and follow the bridleway NE back into Buttermere village. From the village turn L onto the B5289 and follow it NW then N for 3m to the Lanthwaite Wood bridleway. Follow the bridleway W then NW as it descends to the road near Scalehill Bridge. Turn L onto the road and follow it for 1m SW then W to the start of the Loweswater bridleway.

TOUR OF BLENCATHRA

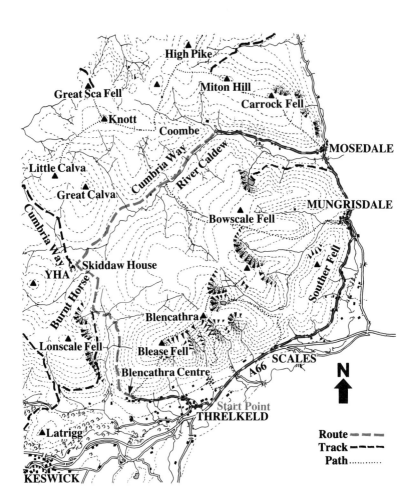

Tour of Blencathra

Grade: Difficult
Time: 4 Hours
Height Gain: 1080ft
Distance: 15 Miles – 6 off road, 9 on road
Terrain: Open moorland and valleys
Surface: Stony, well-graded bridleways and tracks
Start Point Grid Reference: 320254, Threlkeld
Map: O.S. The English Lakes 1:25 000 NE and NW sheets, O.S.
Pathfinder 576 Caldbeck NY 23-33 sheet, O.S. Landranger 90 1:50 000

Blencathra, like its near neighbour, Skiddaw is a particularly striking peak. It sits isolated with its attendant fells and dominates the surrounding valleys. Fine alpine ridges form the southern aspect whilst to the north, rounded fells conceal lonely gills. Also like Skiddaw, Blencathra has a number of bridleways that when linked by roads form an excellent mountain bike tour.

The north side of Blencathra is separated from the Caldbeck Fells by the River Caldew and to the west it is separated from Skiddaw by the Glenderaterra Beck. The valleys of these two water courses are followed by bridleways which meet at Skiddaw House – formerly a shepherd's dwelling, now an 'open' hostel. The bridleway alongside Glenderaterra Beck can be reached by road from Threlkeld. Starting at Threlkeld, and ascending this road first will account for most of the tour's height gain, leaving the long section from Skiddaw House to Mosedale for descent. The whole route is rideable and takes in some splendidly isolated country – the only drawback being a short section on the busy A66.

Route Description

From the centre of Threlkeld take the minor road to Middle Row and the Blencathra Centre as it climbs 1m W. Continue on the road above the Blencathra Centre and pick up the bridleway at the W end of the carpark. Follow the bridleway as it climbs easily W then N above the deeply-cut valley of Glenderaterra Beck. On the other side of the valley are the precipitous crags of Lonscale Fell which are crossed by a bridleway from Latrigg – part of the Tour of Skiddaw. Continue N, crossing numerous fords and follow the bridleway as it swings W. After a short climb the bridleway joins the Latrigg bridleway. Turn R and follow it N, then NW across Burnt Horse to Skiddaw House.

Footbridge over Wiley Gill

From Skiddaw House take the bridleway that descends NE across boggy moorland for ½m to a footbridge over the River Caldew. Cross the river and continue along the bridleway which climbs the other bank. The bridleway continues NE following the River Caldew to a rough carpark and road head after 3½m. This section gives a steady descent – apart from crossing the odd beck.

From the road head follow the pleasant road E to a junction at Mosedale. Turn R and head S for 1½m to Mungrisdale. From Mungrisdale take the Southern Fell road which crosses the bridge out of the village and climbs steadily S then W to join the A66 at Scales – although this road involves some climbing it shortens the time spent on the A66. Join the A66 and follow it W for 2m back to Threlkeld.

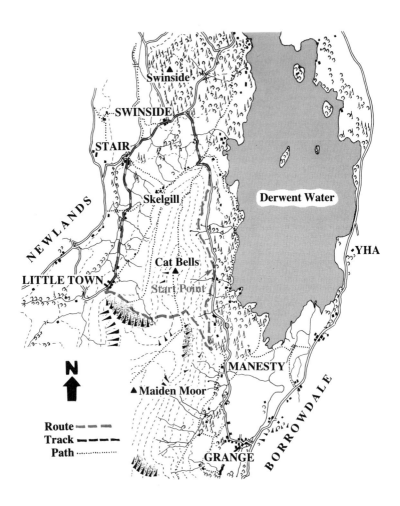

Tour of Cat Bells

Grade: Easy
Time: 1½ Hours
Height Gain: 900ft
Distance: 5½ Miles – 3 off road, 2½ on road
Terrain: Valleys and low fells
Surface: Steep bridleway, pleasant valley roads and terraced track
Start Point Grid Reference: 249197, old quarry near Manesty Park
Maps: O.S. The English Lakes 1:25 000 NW sheet

Cat Bells forms the terminus of a long ridge which separates Borrowdale and Derwent Water from the Newlands Valley. Its shapely summit cone is instantly recognizable as it sits poised above the lovely wooded shores of Derwent Water.

For mountain bikers the main attraction of this little peak is a bridleway which crosses from Manesty on the Derwent Water side to Newlands. It crosses a low point known as Hause Gate just south of Cat Bells' summit. The return trip back to Manesty is made via the pleasant Newlands Valley road to Swinside; then high above the side of Derwent Water utilising the easy bridleway which follows the course of the old Manesty road.

This tour is short and relatively easy, the hardest part being the ascent to Hause Gate – with plenty of stops to admire the view – most people should manage the carry!

Route Description

The Hause Gate bridleway does not come all the way down to the road at Manesty Park as the last short section is footpath. To join the bridleway access needs to be gained at the old quarry at the side of the lake road 1m N of Manesty. From the quarry take the bridleway and follow it S for ¾m as it steadily climbs then drops to a hairpin bend. This is the Hause Gate bridleway. Join it and follow it as it climbs steeply NW to the grassy col of Hause Gate. A short distance N along the ridge is the summit of Cat Bells – it is worth leaving your bike and making the short walk to visit the summit.

From Hause Gate the bridleway descends W into the Newlands Valley. Follow it skirting the rock outcrops of Brunt Crag on their S side. W of Brunt Crag the bridleway becomes rockier and it may be necessary to dismount at the

short scree-run, by the mine workings. This rough section is soon passed and then the good descent can be continued W to a sharp hairpin down into Little Town. Join the valley road at Little Town and follow it N to a junction at Stair. Turn R and follow the road NW to a junction at Swinside. Take the R fork and follow it NW then SE ignoring the turning to Portinscale. After ¾m the road climbs through a steep bend to overlook Derwent Water. Just after this bend a bridleway starts on the R. Take it and follow it back to the start at the quarry.

THE HELVELLYN RANGE COMPLETE

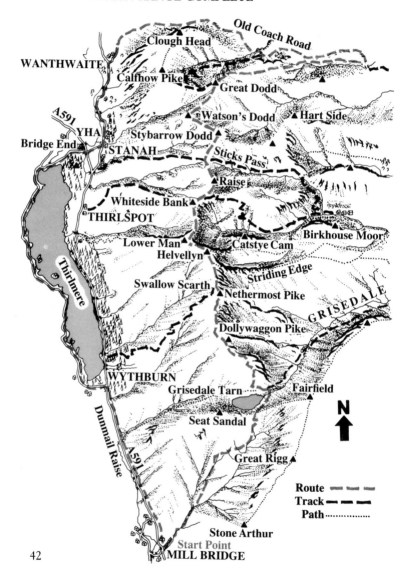

Old Coach Road

Clough Head

WANTHWAITE

Calfhow Pike

Great Dodd

A591

Watson's Dodd · Hart Side

YHA

Stybarrow Dodd

Bridge End

STANAH

Sticks Pass

Raise

Whiteside Bank

THIRLSPOT

Lower Man

Birkhouse Moor

Helvellyn

Catstye Cam

Striding Edge

Thirlmere

Swallow Scarth

Nethermost Pike

GRISEDALE

Dollywaggon Pike

WYTHBURN

Grisedale Tarn

Fairfield

N

Dunmail Raise

Seat Sandal

A591

Great Rigg

Route — — —

Track — —

Path ....

Stone Arthur

Start Point
MILL BRIDGE

Helvellyn Ridge

Grade: Severe
Time: 6½ Hours
Height Gain: 4291ft
Distance: 26 Miles – 16 off road, 10 on road
Terrain: High mountain ridge
Surface: Steep rocky pack-horse road, steep loose ascent, broad open mountain tops, steep narrow ridge encountered in descent, smooth grassy ridge, boggy descent, well-graded coach road and valley roads
Start Point Grid Reference: 336092, Mill Bridge
Maps: O.S. The English Lakes 1:25 000 NE sheet, O.S. Landranger 90

The Helvellyn range without doubt offers some of the best mountain biking in this country. The combination of high mountain terrain and an extensive network of bridleways is virtually unique. Numerous combinations of routes can be worked out with varying levels of difficulty, but by far the most challenging is a complete traverse of the main ridge.

Situated in the north-east corner of the Lake District, the Helvellyn range forms a formidable line of peaks separating Ullswater from Thirlmere. The main ridge runs north to south and maintains a fairly consistent altitude above 2500ft. To the west the slopes are quite uniform only being broken by small rocky outcrops and gills cut by fast-flowing becks. The eastern slopes are a different ball game; alpine ridges separated by deep rocky corries form a spectacular and seemingly impenetrable barrier. To the north of the range the terrain is different again; the peaks become more rounded and grass rather than rock predominates. Completing the traverse from south to north gives the fastest height gain and allows longer descents over gradually moderating terrain.

Route Description

From the A591 at Mill Bridge take the bridleway (old pack-horse road) that climbs NE past a group of houses. Although well-graded the old pack-horse road is none the less very steep climbing straight up Seat Sandal along the course of Little Tongue Gill and only relenting as it contours E then NE to make a final zigzag up to Grisedale Hause. Follow the track over the Hause and down to Grisedale Tarn.

From Grisedale Tarn the work gets even harder. Take the bridleway which zigzags steeply NW up the side of Dollywaggon Pike – the zigzags are steep, loose and unrelenting for nearly 1000ft. The bridleway now heads N giving easy riding as it skirts the summits of both Dollywaggon Pike and Nethermost Pike. Follow it for 1m to Swallow Scarth – a dramatically positioned col. From Swallow Scarth another easy ½m riding leads N, directly to Helvellyn's summit and its attendant Shelter.

Cross the summit plateau in a NW direction, passing the path which descends to Swirral Edge (marked by a cairn) and then make for the cairn of Lower Man. In poor visibility the route to Lower Man is very confusing – from the trig point on Helvellyn follow a bearing of 295° (grid) for 500yds then 340° for 100yds to the cairn. From Lower Man the route follows a steep narrow ridge N down to the col above Brown Cove. This ridge is the crux of the whole route and can be very exciting; a fall here could have serious consequences – great care should be taken. If in doubt get off and walk! Continue N across the col and ascend the slopes of Whiteside Bank. The fells to the E become less steep and the track along the ridge less distinct, so when leaving Whiteside Bank make sure you take the right route, which is to the NE. The going is easy over grass and small loose stones, with the occasional bigger rock to get you out of the saddle. The ascent to Raise is not too steep but will quicken your breathing enough to make you appreciate a rest on top. From Raise continue N and drop down to Sticks Pass.

Once past Raise, the main bulk of the Helvellyn range lies behind; the route lies to the N with a steep climb to Stybarrow Dodd. The climb is smooth and just about rideable – a real muscle buster! From Stybarrow Dodd (not the trig point) easy riding leads NW for ¾m to Watson's Dodd with some overall height loss. Level riding NE then a short pull leads to the last high point of the route: Great Dodd at 2807ft.

From Great Dodd a bridleway is taken that descends NE across Matterdale Common and joins the Old Coach Road at Groove Beck. From the summit, the bridleway is followed steeply N for ⅓m, then NE as it eases to give a 2m descent – some sections alongside Groove Beck are boggy and should be walked.

The Old Coach Road maintains a consistent height as it skirts Matterdale Common and Clough Head giving excellent riding. Generally the going is easy but there are some boggy sections and a couple of climbs.

From the footbridge at Groovebeck Fold join the Old Coach Road and follow it first N then W. Continue W, skirting Threlkeld Knotts on its northern side. The last 2m section down to the B5322 at Wanthwaite is steep and very fast.

From Wanthwaite take the B5322 S down St. John's in the Vale to Stanah and a junction with the A591. The A591 can be taken straight back to Mill Bridge but it is quieter and more interesting to take the minor road around the west bank of Thirlmere. Turn R onto the A591 and back-track N for ½m to pick up the lake road at the first L. The lake road is followed S for 5m to rejoin the A591 at Wythburn. Turn R and head S as the road climbs to Dunmail Raise. The pull up Dunmail Raise is rewarded by a 2m free-wheel back to the start.

44

MOOR DIVOCK

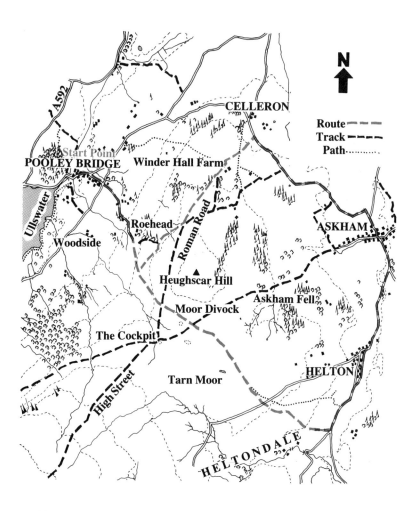

Moor Divock

Grade: Easy
Time: 1½ Hours
Height Gain: 925ft
Distance: 9 Miles – 5 off road, 4 on road
Terrain: Moorland and low fells
Surface: Well-graded access tracks, lanes and quiet roads
Start Point Grid Reference: 472244, Pooley Bridge
Maps: O.S. The English Lakes 1:25 000 NE sheet

At the northern end of the High Street range the moorland plateau of Moor Divock provides an extensive selection of mountain bike rides. This wide, open moorland is liberally criss-crossed by clear, easy to follow bridleways with no serious obstacles and no inclines steep enough to force a carry – ideal for venue beginners.

The route described crosses Moor Divock from Pooley Bridge, at the head of Ullswater, to Askham on the River Lowther and returns via peaceful country roads and the flanks of Heughscar Hill. This is only one of a number of possible variations and, as such, is a good introduction to the area, after which other equally enjoyable routes can be explored.

On Moor Divock there are a number of important historical sights including ancient cairns, avenues, burial mounds, settlements, standing stones and of course 'High Street' – the Roman road: all of which are well worth investigating. Be careful not to cause any damage and do not stray from the bridleways with your bike.

Route Description

From the centre of Pooley Bridge take the minor road that leads SE to Roehead. Go straight across the cross-roads and continue SE for ½m up the lane to the start of a bridleway at Roehead. Pass through the gate and follow the good bridleway as it climbs slowly SE to a cairn and signpost. Continue SE from the signpost as the bridleway levels to another signpost after ¼m. This is Moor Divock, the highest point on the route.

From Moor Divock two bridleways head E: one NE towards Askham and one SE towards Helton and Bampton (via minor roads). Take the Helton/Bampton bridleway which gives a good descent for 1m to a minor road, which it crosses, then continues to descend SE for a further ¾m along a lane to a junction. Turn L at the junction and follow the minor road N for 2m through Helton to

Askham. Continue N on the minor road from Askham to a fork. Take the L branch and follow it as it winds its way NW to the start of a bridleway on the L after 1½m – opposite a quarry.

This bridleway is part of High Street and access is via Winder Hall Farm. Take the bridleway and follow it past the farm. Just after the farm the bridleway forks. Take the R branch and follow it SW across rough pasture. After ½m the bridleway crosses a good track. Turn R onto the track and follow it to a fork. At the fork take the L branch which climbs slightly then descends SW to join the Roehead bridleway. Turn R onto the bridleway and descend NE back to Roehead. From Roehead retrace the route along the road to Pooley Bridge.

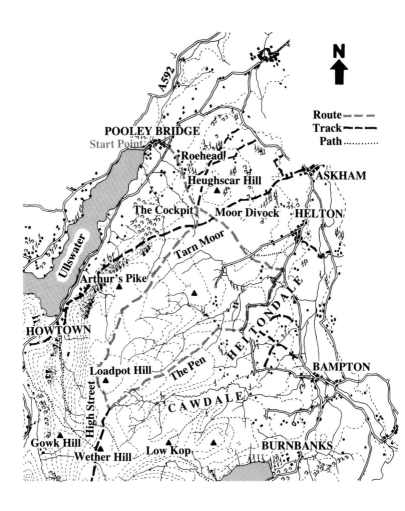

Loadpot Hill

Grade: Very Difficult
Time: 3½-4 Hours
Height Gain: 2001ft
Distance: 13 Miles – 10 off road, 3 on road
Terrain: Rounded hills and moorland
Surface: Well-graded access track, boggy moorland, grassy exposed fells and fell roads
Start Point Grid Reference: 472244, Pooley Bridge
Maps: O.S. The English Lakes 1:25 000 NE sheet

Loadpot Hill is the last main summit on the end of the High Street ridge before it begins its northerly descent. This vantage point provides unrestricted views: west over Ullswater and east towards Lowther and the Eden Valley. It also marks the junction of a bridleway from Heltondale with the bridleway along High Street.

The Heltondale bridleway makes a particularly good descent starting with a fine traverse across the head of Heltondale then breaking out onto open fellside with a fast run down a grassy track. The ascent up the High Street bridleway, although a bit of a pull, is as equally rewarding giving a surprising amount of riding on good, clear ground.

This route crosses Moor Divock, a moorland plateau north of Loadpot Hill, on which there are a number of important historical sights including ancient cairns, avenues, burial mounds, settlements and standing stones: all of which are well worth investigating, but be careful not to cause any damage and do not stray from the bridleways with your bike.

Route Description

From the centre of Pooley Bridge take the minor road that leads SE for ½m up the lane to the start of a bridleway at Roehead. Pass through the gate and follow the good bridleway as it climbs slowly SE to a cairn and signpost. At the cairn and signpost turn R for 'High Street' and follow the bridleway S over boggy ground to a ford near the Cockpit – a stone circle. Cross the ford and follow the bridleway as it heads W a short distance to a fork. The R branch descends to Howtown. Ignore it and take the L branch which climbs steadily up the fellside. Follow it for 4m, first SW then S as it steepens and swings around the summit of Loadpot Hill to a col. If you want to visit the summit trig point you will have to leave your bike at the col.

The descent starts from the col by following the Heltondale bridleway across

Cop Stone

the SE slopes of Loadpot Hill. Take the bridleway from the col and follow it NE along a terrace for 1m until it breaks out onto the open moorland of The Pen. The Pen is really a broad spur which extends NE. Once on it the bridleway becomes a little indistinct, but basically follows its N side. The going is not particularly difficult at any point of this section so if you lose the bridleway, continue NE for 2m until the bridleway becomes clear again above the intake wall. Follow the bridleway NE alongside the wall until it turns E by a barn onto a track. Follow the track E to the minor road. Turn L onto the road and follow it as it winds its way N then NE for 1½m to a junction. At the junction take the first L and follow the lane as it climbs NW ¾m to a minor road. Cross directly over the road and pick up the Moor Divock bridleway on the other side. Follow the bridleway as it climbs easily NW onto Moor Divock. After 1m a junction and signpost is reached. Continue NW as the bridleway starts to descend for ½m until the same cairn and signpost seen at the start of the ride is reached. Retrace the route and make the fast descent NE to Roehead and then back to Pooley Bridge.

Tour of Place Fell

Grade: Difficult
Time: 2 Hours
Height Gain: 850ft
Distance: 8 Miles – 6 off road, 2 on road
Terrain: Mountain pass and lake shore
Surface: Steep but generally well-graded mountain tracks and a stony lake-side bridleway
Start Point Grid Reference: 398158, Patterdale
Maps: O.S. The English Lakes 1:25 000 NE sheet

Boredale occupies a rather secretive and isolated position behind Place Fell and east of Ullswater. The road, from the north, into the dale climbs a tortuous little pass and as this road is a cul-de-sac it attracts few people and little traffic. The only other route into Boredale is via a bridleway from Patterdale which crosses the southern ridge of Place Fell at Boredale Hause. Originally this bridleway was the link between the two communities, being the most direct, either mounted or on foot, but as with many other 'Social Roads' the advent of motor transport has seen its use diminish. As a mountain bike ride this route is ideal. The bridleway is well-graded throughout its length – although some carrying will be necessary on the ascent from Patterdale to Boredale Hause. Once Boredale is gained a return trip can be made via the pleasant bridleway which skirts the eastern shores of Ullswater. This bridleway is a popular route for walkers and has many blind corners and summits, so care should be taken.

Route Description

Just S of Patterdale on the A592 a side road crosses Goldrill Beck. Take it and follow it NW then N for ⅓m to the start of the bridleway to Boredale Hause. The bridleway climbs SE across the flanks of Place Fell to finally swing E as it attains Boredale Hause after ¾m. This section of the route is the main height gain and although the bridleway is in good order the steeper sections may dictate some carrying. Boredale Hause is a broad open col with a number of tracks and paths that radiate from it. The bridleway to Boredale heads NE and crosses a low grass bluff – a vague path to start. Once the bridleway crosses the bluff and starts to descend it becomes more clear on the ground.

The first section of the descent is through a steep zigzag which can prove

quite testing in wet conditions; next is a superb terrace which gives a steep but well-graded run down into Boredale. The descent leads NE for 1m to Boredale Head – a farm. Pass through the farmyard and pick up the valley road. Follow the road for 1¼m now heading NE, to a junction. At the junction take the L fork and follow it round to Sandwick where a bridleway along the shores of Ullswater can be picked up. This is followed as it works its way across the crags and becks above the lake to Side Farm. Continue past Side Farm to join the lane back to the A592.

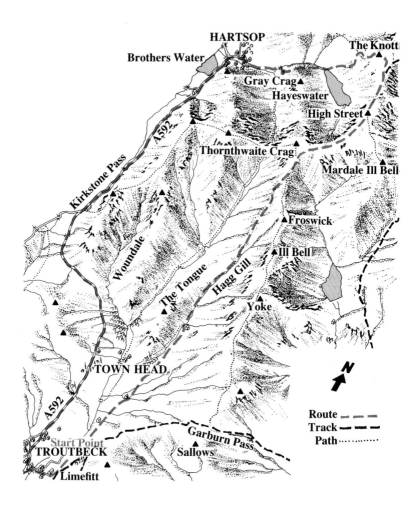

HARTSOP

Brothers Water

The Knott ▲

Gray Crag ▲

Hayeswater

High Street ▲

A592

Kirkstone Pass

Thornthwaite Crag

Mardale Ill Bell ▲

Froswick ▲

Woundale

Ill Bell ▲

The Tongue

Hagg Gill

Yoke ▲

TOWN HEAD

N

A592

Route - - -
Track — —
Path ⋯⋯

Garburn Pass

Start Point
TROUTBECK

Sallows ▲

Limefitt ▲

High Street South

Grade: Severe
Time: 5 Hours
Height Gain: 3320ft
Distance: 16 Miles – 8½ off road, 7½ on road
Terrain: High mountains
Surface: Busy road pass, well-graded access track, smooth grassy ridge and a rocky bridleway
Start Point Grid Reference: 413036, A592 at Troutbeck on SE sheet
Maps: O.S. The English Lakes 1:25 000 SE and NE sheets, O.S. Landranger 90 1:50 000

The southern section of High Street gives one of the best mountain bike descents in the Lake District. From the summit of High Street to Troutbeck, the height loss is in the order of 2300 feet over 5½ miles – most of it in the first 2½ miles! The going is excellent all the way over well-graded tracks, for which we can thank the Roman road builders. Only at a couple of spots on the steep flanks of Froswick will the more cautious be tempted to dismount.

Such fine descents do not come easily. Access to High Street from Troutbeck is hard won, first by the slog up Kirkstone Pass, then by the steep carry to High Street from the lovely hamlet of Hartsop.

Route Description

From Troutbeck join the A592 and follow it as it climbs steadily for 3¾m first N and then NW and finally N again to the top of the Kirkstone Pass (Kirkstone Pass Inn). The route now can be followed on the NE sheet. From the top follow the road for 3½m as it descends steeply N passing Brothers Water to the Hartsop turning (just over Horseman Bridge). Turn R and follow the lane to Hartsop. From Hartsop take the well-graded access track that crosses, and then follows Hayeswater Gill on the R bank to a ford 200yds downstream of the Water Board dam at Hayeswater (if you do not fancy wet feet there is a bridge just below the dam). Take the zigzags that climb E up to The Knott and join the path from Angle Tarn before the last pull around the summit. From the col behind The Knott ride easily S for 1m along the course of High Street to the summit of High Street, also known as Racecourse Hill (trig point slightly off the track). The track is clear and should be stuck to

especially in mist as there are crags to the W and E.

From High Street follow the course of the 'Roman Road' SW across the broad col below Thornthwaite Crag. (Change back to the SE sheet). After 1m the track starts to steepen and descends a narrowing ridge – this is the start of the descent proper. Ignore the path to Froswick, this descends to the col. Instead follow the track that forks R and SW. The track rapidly steepens but is well-graded and gives an exhilarating descent across the western slopes of Froswick down to Hagg Gill. Once the intake wall is reached, the gradient eases considerably. Continue along the track which heads generally S and follow it for 1m to a fork. Take the L branch across the bridge. Over the bridge continue S along the track as it slowly descends and finally climbs for 2½m to a fork above the camp-site at Limefitt Park. Take the R fork and follow the bridleway down through the camp-site and back to the A592 at Troutbeck.

Thornthwaite Beacon

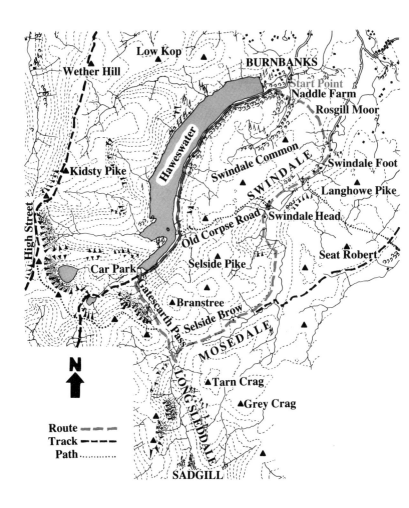

Low Kop

Wether Hill

BURNBANKS

Start Point

Naddle Farm

Rosgill Moor

Kidsty Pike

Swindale Common

Swindale Foot

SWINDALE

Langhowe Pike

High Street

Old Corpse Road

Swindale Head

Car Park

Selside Pike

Seat Robert

Gatescarth Pass

Branstree

Selside Brow

MOSEDALE

N

Tarn Crag

Grey Crag

LONG SLEDDALE

Route — — —
Track — — —
Path ....

SADGILL

Haweswater and Swindale

Grade: Difficult
Time: 4 Hours
Height Gain: 1755ft
Distance: 12½ Miles – 6½ off road, 6 on road
Terrain: Mountain passes
Surface: Valley roads and well-graded pack-horse roads, boggy in parts
Start Point Grid Reference: 509157, Haweswater road, Naddle Farm turning, NE sheet
Maps: O.S. The English Lakes 1:25 000 NE and SE sheets, O.S. Landranger 90 1:50 000

Mardale and Swindale are situated between the High Street range of fells and Shap. One of the original links between these two dales was via the old corpse road that crosses directly over Mardale Common. In its hey-day the old corpse road would have been a pack-horse route, but unfortunately modern classification has it defined as a footpath rather than a bridleway: a strange logic which renders it out of bounds to bicycles.

To tour these two lovely valleys on mountain bikes means making use of the slightly more circuitous routes at their heads. Crossing at the western ends of the valleys is a bridleway over Gatescarth Pass and the Mosedale Watershed which provides exciting, if boggy, mountain biking. At the eastern ends of the valleys a shorter and certainly drier route crosses through the charming glades and fells of Naddle and Rosgill Moor.

Route Description

Starting at the Naddle Farm turning follow the Haweswater road SW for 4½m along Mardale to its terminus at the carpark. From the carpark take the bridleway and follow it W a short distance to a fork. (Change to the SE sheet). Take the L branch and follow it as it swings round to the SE and starts to steepen. This is the Gatescarth Pass bridleway and climbs to the top of the pass in 1m. Continue SE across the col and follow the bridleway as it descends into Longsleddale. The descent can be very boggy having been badly eroded by motorbikes and four-wheel drive vehicles. After ½m join the old quarry road. A short distance along this is a junction. Turn L onto the bridleway that climbs to a col at Selside Brow. Follow the vague and boggy bridleway NE for ¾m to the fence at the col.

Once across the col the bridleway starts to descend. Follow it NE for 1m to Mosedale Cottage. (Change back to the NE sheet). After Mosedale Cottage the bridleway improves and becomes easier to follow. Continue NE along it for ⅓m to a fork at a ford. Take the L branch and follow it as it skirts the fellside high above Mosedale Beck. Continue NE then N for 1m to a broad spur at the head of Swindale. Follow the vague bridleway across the spur. As it begins to descend into Swindale it becomes more distinct. Descend NW through the steep zigzags, then N, and join the road at Swindale Head. From Swindale Head take the road NE for 1½m to the start of a bridleway on the left.

The bridleway climbs the steep fellside of Rosgill Moor then descends into Mardale. Turn L onto the bridleway and climb it NE for ½m to a broad col – the bridleway is vague at first, but soon becomes more distinct after 200yds. Continue NW across the col and pick up the good track that swings W and descends through woodland to Naddle Farm. Go through the farmyard and follow the farm track N back to the Haweswater Road.

Swindale Head Farm.

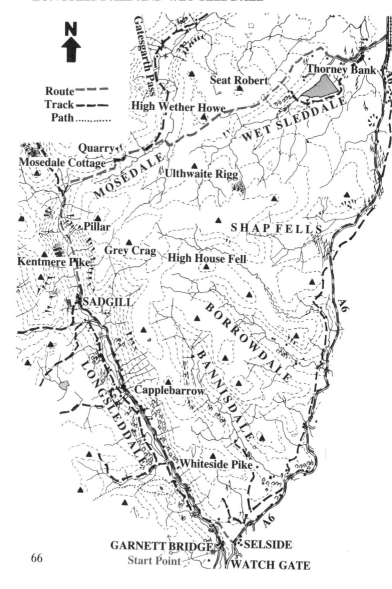

N

Route-- --
Track-- --
Path...........

Gatesgarth Pass

Thorney Bank

Seat Robert

High Wether Howe

WET SLEDDALE

Quarry

Mosedale Cottage

MOSEDALE

Ulthwaite Rigg

SHAP FELLS

Pillar

Grey Crag

High House Fell

Kentmere Pike

SADGILL

BORROWDALE

BANNISDALE

A6

Capplebarrow

LONGSLEDDALE

Whiteside Pike

A6

GARNETT BRIDGE   SELSIDE
Start Point   WATCH GATE

Longsleddale and Wet Sleddale

Grade: Difficult
Time: 5½ Hours
Height Gain: 2129ft
Distance: 24 Miles – 9 off road, 15 on road
Terrain: Valleys and high moorland
Surface: Pleasant valley roads, old quarry road, pack-horse road, boggy bridleways, rocky tracks and road pass
Start Point Grid Reference: 523992, Garnett Bridge, SE sheet
Maps: O.S. The English Lakes 1:25 000 SE and NE sheets, Landranger 90 and 97 1:50 000

The Shap Fells occupy the easternmost part of the Lake District National Park. Separating these fells from the rest of the Lake District are the valleys of Longsleddale and Wet Sleddale. The bleak fells contained within this area are some of the loneliest in Lakeland: there is little habitation and the fells themselves are rounded and have a distinctly blasted feel to them. Although lacking the picturesque charm associated with the rest of Lakeland, they nevertheless have their own uniquely peaceful atmosphere.

Longsleddale is serviced first by a narrow road, then by an old quarry road and finally by a bridleway. This route connects with the bridleway along Wet Sleddale via the upper reaches of Mosedale. Following this route on a mountain bike is a considerable undertaking, not because the ground it covers is particularly difficult (though it does have its moments) but more because the route which links the ends of each valley is quite long – it entails following the A6 over Shap.

Route Description

From Garnett Bridge follow the Longsleddale road NW for 5m to Sadgill. Past Sadgill the road begins to deteriorate into a track and heads N. Continue along for 2m to a junction. The first part climbs slowly but soon steepens until it eases again at the junction. The L fork heads NW to the Gatesgarth Pass. Ignore this – take the R branch that climbs to a col at Selside Brow. Follow the vague and boggy bridleway NE for ¾m to the fence. Once across the col the bridleway starts to descend. Follow it NE for 1m to Mosedale Cottage. After Mosedale Cottage the bridleway improves and becomes easier to follow.

Continue NE along for ⅓m to a fork at a ford. Take the R fork and follow it alongside Mosedale Beck to a bridge. Cross the bridge and follow the vague course of the old cart track as it zigzags NE up the fellside. After ½m the track opens out onto a broad open col – this is the head of Wet Sleddale. (Change to NE sheet).

Continue NE across the col. This section is a little frustrating as the col is so wide and the track is not very clear on the ground. After ½m the descent finally begins and the track becomes more clear. Follow it as it skirts NE on the N side of Wet Sleddale 2½m to a bend at the corner of a wall – there are numerous tracks leading off to the R – ignore them and stick with the main track. At the bend the track swings SE. Follow it down through pasture to join the road at Thorney Bank. Join the road and follow it NE to a T junction. At the T junction turn L and continue NE to another T junction with the A6.

Join the A6 and follow it S. (Change to SE sheet). The first 5m are a bit of a slog after which an eye-watering descent leads in a further 6m to the start of a bridleway at Selside. Turn R onto the bridleway and follow it NW first along a lane then down through pleasant pasture to join the Longsleddale road. Turn L and follow the road SW back to Garnett Bridge.

Mosedale Cottage.

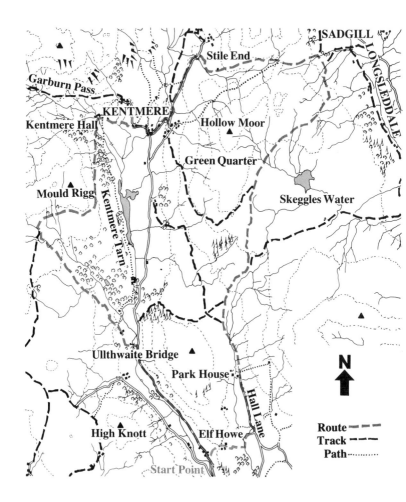

Tour of Kentmere

Grade: Moderate
Time: 3 Hours
Height Gain: 1532ft
Distance: 10½ Miles – 7½ off road, 3 on road
Terrain: Low fells and exposed moorland
Surface: Stony pack-horse tracks, valley roads and rough moorland
Start point Grid Reference: 466996, Kentmere valley road near Elf Howe
Maps: O.S. The English Lakes 1:25 000 SE sheet

Of all the valleys in the Lake District, Kentmere has probably the highest density of rights of way open to mountain bikers. All but a handful of the routes are either bridleways or tracks of higher status. Routes such as Garburn Pass, Nan Bield Pass and Stile End are all well established as popular classics offering mountain biking of the highest quality. Of equal quality are those routes within the bounds of Kentmere itself – allowing extensive off-road riding.

This tour takes in both sides of the Kentmere valley and makes a detour to the top of Stile End Pass to overlook Longsleddale. Although not strictly within the boundary of Kentmere, this detour gives access to the high and secluded moorland of the Green Quarter and provides an excellent descent past Skeggles Water and then along Hall Lane. The bridleways of the Green Quarter are extensively used by the Equestrian Centre at Park House – care should be taken when passing horses.

Route Description

The start of this route is on the valley road 250yds past Scroggs Bridge, on the E side of the River Kent at a junction with a bridleway – parking in Kentmere is difficult, particularly in summer so it is worth parking in Staveley and cycling the short section of road to the start point. From the start point follow the valley road NW 1¼m to Ullthwaite Bridge. Turn L and follow the bridleway over the bridge. After the bridge follow the bridleway as it swings round to the NW and then starts to climb along a stony lane. After ¼m the lane splits. Take the L fork and follow the lane as it opens out onto the fell side and continues NW. Climbing for 1m, the bridleway crosses Black Beck then Park Beck to a junction with a bridleway. Join the bridleway and follow it N then E

alongside the wall. The bridleway then swings N to give a good descent to Kentmere Hall. From Kentmere Hall take the lane E to Kentmere village.

From the church, head E then S along the valley road and cross Low Bridge. Turn sharp L and climb the road to Green Quarter. Turn L again and follow the road to a fork. Take the R branch for ½m to a R turn onto a track. Follow the track as it steadily climbs past Stile End and works its way to the top of the pass. Continue along the track as it makes a steep, rocky descent into Longsleddale. After ⅓m turn R and cross a beck to pick up a bridleway. Follow the bridleway alongside the wall as it climbs S and then SW onto rough open moorland. The bridleway is vague across the moorland and reaches a high point after 1m overlooking Skeggles Water and Cocklaw Fell. From the high point descend SW for ¾m to a fork. Take the L branch – the R branch climbs then descends to Kentmere village. Head S along the gradually improving bridleway for 1¾m to Park House and join Hall Lane. Follow Hall Lane S for ½m to a bridleway. Turn R onto the bridleway and follow it down to Hall Beck and then onto a bridge. Cross the bridge and follow the lane W through Elf Howe and then SW to the valley road and the start.

Bridge near Elf Howe.

WINDERMERE AND CROOK

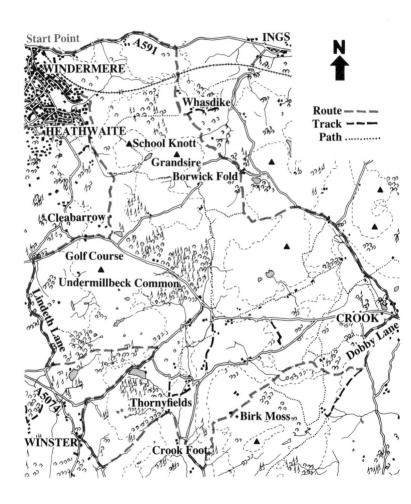

Windermere and Crook

Grade: Easy
Time: 3 Hours
Height Gain: 910ft
Distance: 14 Miles – 6½ off road, 7½ on road
Terrain: Low wooded fells and pasture
Surface: Roads, bridleways over pasture and green lanes
Start Point Grid Reference: 413987 Windermere railway station
Maps: O.S. The English Lakes 1:25 000 SE sheet

The towns of Windermere and Bowness back onto a lovely little group of fells that extend east towards Stavely and Crook. None of the summits have a particularly memorable shape and only a few exceed the 700 foot contour. Regardless of their modest proportions, they are still probably the most viewed summits in the Lake District. This is due entirely to their proximity to the A591 which forms their northern boundary and carries most traffic into and out of the National Park.

Amongst these fells are numerous hamlets and villages which are interlinked by lanes and bridleways. Some of the lanes have been adopted as roads but many still retain their original form as green lanes. Generally they provide easy mountain biking and are a good option when the weather is too hot for a slog over the tops or passes.

Most of the route described is clear on the ground and is well signposted, but there are a number of sections through enclosed farmland – if you are unsure about the course of a right of way – ask, most of the local farmers are very obliging.

Route Description

From Windermere railway station join the A591 and follow it E for 1¼m to a turning on the R. Turn R onto the narrow road and follow it S over the railway bridge past Blackmoss to a fork. Take the R branch and continue S to a bend. Follow the road round the bend to a junction. Turn R and follow the road SE to a T junction. At the junction turn L and follow the road for 400yds to Borwick Fold.

At Borwick Fold join the bridleway and follow it around the short lane and

75

then S as it climbs across pasture. After ⅓m the bridleway forks. Take the L branch and follow it as it swings round to the E and descends to join a minor road. Turn R onto the road and follow it SE for 1½m to Crook. At Crook turn R onto the B5284 then first L onto Dobby Lane, which is followed SW to a T junction. Turn L and follow the road S for ¼m to a track on the R. Join the track and follow it SW a short distance to a fork. Take the R branch and follow it to another fork at a gate. Go through the gate and take the L branch W alongside a wall to a T junction on a farm track. Turn L and follow the track SW across pasture (vague) to a bridge after ¼m. Go over the bridge and continue SW along the side of the field to join the farm track at the other side. Continue SW along the track through the dog-leg to the farm at Birk Moss. Follow the bridleway around the farm then SW over a short rise to a T junction. Turn L onto the good track and descend S along it to join the Crosthwaite road.

At the road turn R and follow it NW for ⅓m to a bridleway on the L. Take the bridleway and follow it past Crook Foot then N to Thornyfields. At Thornyfields turn L in front of the houses then join the bridleway behind the barn. The bridleway climbs SW to a low col. Follow it over the col and continue SW to join the A5074. Turn R onto the A5074 and follow it NW to Winster. At Winster turn R in front of the pub and follow the minor road as it climbs to a T junction. Turn R at the junction and follow the road as it climbs NE for ¾m to a lane on the L. Join the lane and follow it as it climbs W. The gradient soon eases to give a good run down to a junction with Lindeth Lane.

Turn R onto Lindeth Lane and follow it as it winds its way N for 1¼m to the junction on the B5284. Turn R and follow the B5284 E for ¾m to a lane on the L – by the side of a tarn. Follow the lane then bridleway N for 1¼m to a bridge. Cross the bridge and then head NW through the Droomer housing estate – there are numerous routes which lead into Windermere. Once in Windermere follow the one-way system back to the railway station.

GREENUP EDGE AND BLEA TARN

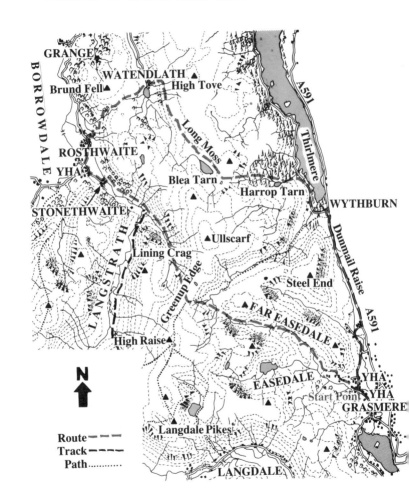

Greenup Edge and Blea Tarn

Grade: Very Difficult
Time: 5 Hours
Height Gain: 3500ft
Distance: 16 Miles – 10 off road, 6 on road
Terrain: High mountain passes
Surface: Busy road pass, steep rocky bridleways and broad mountain ridges with boggy sections
Start Point Grid Reference: 337076, Grasmere, SE sheet
Maps: O.S. The English Lakes 1:25 000 SE and NW sheets, Landranger 90 1:50 000

Running north from the Langdale Pikes, a long line of fells separates Borrowdale from Grasmere and Thirlmere. Crossing this high watershed are two old packhorse routes: one over the southern half at Greenup Edge, and the other over the northern half at Blea Tarn. Greenup Edge is the higher of the two, attaining a maximum altitude of 1995ft at a wild and exposed col between High Raise and Ullscarf. It is also probably the harder of the two crossings, though there is little in it. The Blea Tarn crossing is a little lower at 1665ft but its technical sections are just as testing and not without interest!

On the Thirlmere and Grasmere side there is little alternative but to make use of the busy A591 over Dunmail Raise as a link. On the Borrowdale side, however, there is a pleasant bridleway between Watendlath and Rosthwaite with a fine descent on the Rosthwaite side – which, when combined with the cracking descents from Greenup Edge and Blea Tarn, will more than make up for the frustration of the boulders, bogs and carrying.

Route Description

From Grasmere take the Easedale road and follow it NW for ½m to a junction just past Goody Bridge. At the junction turn R and follow the road N to a T junction. Turn L and follow the road through Town Head to the A591. Turn L onto the A591 and follow it N over Dunmail Raise to a junction at Wythburn. (NW sheet). Turn L onto the Armboth road and follow it around the end of Thirlmere for 1m to the start of a bridleway on the L. This bridleway leads to Harrop Tarn and then onto Blea Tarn. Take it and follow it as it zigzags then climbs generally W through woodland to the ford at Harrop Tarn.

Cross the ford (stepping stones) and follow the bridleway W for just over ½m through woodland to a deer fence at its edge. Go through the gate and continue W as the bridleway climbs steeply across open fell to a broad col overlooking Blea Tarn.

From the col the bridleway heads NW above Blea Tarn descending slowly over very boggy ground. After 1½m the ground becomes dryer and the riding more enjoyable. Continue NW for a further ½m along the bridleway as it traverses high above Bleatarn Gill, with numerous rock steps on route. The bridleway then turns sharp L and descends steeply through a series of well-graded zigzags. Follow it down to the lovely little hamlet at Watendlath – farmhouse café for refreshments.

From Watendlath take the bridleway that heads W over the Grange Fells to Rosthwaite. The first section is a short climb up a stony track to a col overlooking Borrowdale. From the col make the fine descent down to Rosthwaite. Pick up the valley road and follow it S for ½m to the Stonethwaite road. Turn L onto it and follow it for another ½m into Stonethwaite.

From Stonethwaite turn L and take the Greenup Edge bridleway that crosses Stonethwaite Beck and then follows it SE to its confluence with Greenup Gill and Langstrath Beck. Continue SE and follow Greenup Gill as it climbs SE for 2m. At first the going is not too bad but it soon starts to deteriorate, becoming very rough. The gradient only relents once Lining Crag is passed and the bridleway opens out onto the broad col of Greenup Edge.

From Greenup Edge, paths head SW to High Raise and NE to Ullscarf. These should not be confused with the bridleway that heads SE – particularly in poor visibility. Descend SE along the boggy bridleway and cross the head waters of Wythburn to another lower col. This col is the true head of Far Easedale and marks the start of a testing descent. The impressive crags to the S are Deer Bields Buttress. The bridleway heads E then SE for 2½m to a group of houses at Kitty Crag. From Kitty Crag join the Easedale Road and follow it for 1m as it pleasantly winds its way SE into Grasmere.

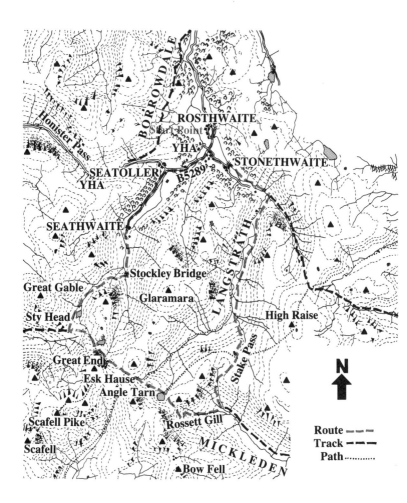

Esk Hause and Stake Pass

Grade: Severe
Time: 5½ Hours
Height Gain: 3326ft
Distance: 14 Miles – 10½ off road, 3½ on road
Terrain: High mountain passes
Surface: Rough valley tracks, steep rocky mountain passes and valley roads
Start Point Grid Reference: 258149, Rosthwaite, NW sheet
Maps: O.S. The English Lakes 1:25 000 NW and SW sheets, O.S. Landranger 90 1:50 000

The bulk of Lakeland's mountains lie around Esk Hause and from this central hub of peaks the valleys of Borrowdale, Eskdale, Langdale and Wasdale radiate like spokes of a huge wheel. Esk Hause itself is rather innocuous being a broad, rocky col with little to distinguish it save a few cairns and the shelter on its north-eastern side. Its claim to fame is as an important cross-roads of bridleways and paths which give access to the magnificent heights that surround it.

Crossing Esk Hause (by the shelter) is a bridleway that links Langdale with Borrowdale and Wasdale. Following its course on a mountain bike is a serious undertaking, comparable with any of the other harder mountain bike routes in the Lake District. In addition other sections which, if included, make the route a circular tour are only a little easier than that described above: these being via Sty Head from Borrowdale and Stake Pass from Langstrath. The combination of these routes offers a considerable challenge that will demand good mountain skills and a degree of stamina – the rewards, however, are plenty with a passage through some of this country's finest mountains.

Route Description

Head S out of Rosthwaite on the B5289 for ½m to a junction. Turn L and follow the road to Stonethwaite. From Stonethwaite turn L and pick up the bridleway that crosses Stonethwaite Bridge. The bridleway heads SE alongside Stonethwaite Beck towards Greenup Edge. After 1m the bridleway forks. Ignore the Greenup Edge branch and take the R branch over a bridge. On the other side follow the bridleway SW for 2¼m alongside Langstrath Beck to a

bridge across Stake Beck – the going is surprisingly rough for such an easy gradient. From the bridge the climbing starts in earnest. (Change to SW sheet). Follow the steep rocky zigzags SE then SW for ¾m to the top of Stake Pass. The descent from Stake Pass down into Mickleden valley at the head of Langdale is a real delight: unfortunately it is over all too soon. Descend SW then S through the well-graded zigzags for 1m to a junction with the bridleway from Langdale.

At the junction turn R onto the bridleway and follow it W up Rosset Gill. The first section climbs steadily for ½m to a vague junction. This junction was caused by the reinstatement of the original pack-horse route. The R branch was caused by walkers short-cutting the pack-horse route and scrambling up the side of Rosset Gill, causing some erosion. Take the L branch and follow it as it snakes its way W then NW to the head of Rosset Gill – this section is easy to follow as it has recently been pitched.

From the head of Rosset Gill continue NW for 1m past Angle Tarn to Esk Hause shelter. From the shelter the bridleway continues to head NW passing under the crags of Great End and alongside Sprinkling Tarn for 1½m to the Mountain Rescue Box at Sty Head. Facing NE and being at a relatively high altitude, Great End holds snow longer than any other crag in the Lake District, save perhaps those on Helvellyn. The gullies provide excellent middle grade winter climbs and have produced considerable avalanches. If crossing this section in mist take care not to take the Grains Gill path: this heads N and can be easily identified by the gorge at its head.

Sty Head is also an important access point to the surrounding peaks with numerous paths and tracks heading off in all directions. From the Mountain Rescue Box head NE over boggy ground until you pick up a stony track past Styhead Tarn. Continue NE and follow the course of Sty Head Gill first on the L bank and then, after a bridge, on the R bank with rough going through boulders to a small wood above Taylorgill Force. (Change to NW sheet). The track now leaves the Gill and heads steeply down the fell side to Stockley Bridge. From Stockley Bridge take the good track N to Seathwaite and then the road for 1½m back to Seatoller. From the T junction at Seatoller turn R and follow the B5289 E then N back to Rosthwaite.

LOUGHRIGG TERRACE, TILBERTHWAITE AND CLAIFE HEIGHTS

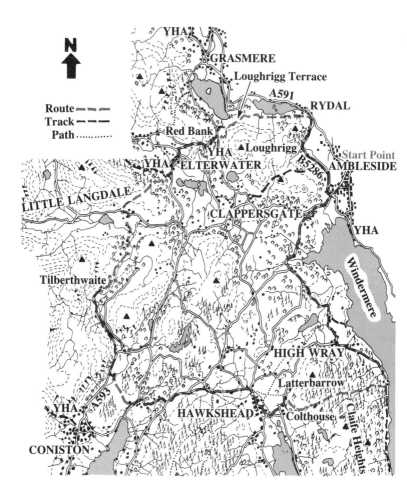

Loughrigg Terrace, Tilberthwaite and Claife Heights

Grade: Moderate
Time: 4½ Hours
Height Gain: 1653ft
Distance: 20½ Miles – 8 off road, 12½ on road
Terrain: Low wooded fells
Surface: Roads, quarry tracks and well-graded bridleways
Start Point Grid Reference: 376044, Ambleside
Maps: O.S. The English Lakes 1:25 000 SE sheet

The fells and dales encircled by Ambleside, Coniston and Grasmere epitomise the Lake District for most people. The combination of pretty little hamlets with tea rooms and pubs, plenty of water for sailing and fishing and wooded fells with easy walking and an occasional glimpse of the higher peaks have proved to be a real honey pot for trippers. Throughout the summer and on bank holidays the area is best avoided, but out of season it gives good mountain biking amongst superb scenery – particularly in autumn when the range of colours in the trees are magnificent.

There are many off-road routes, either bridleways or tracks of higher status, criss-crossing the area. Some are old pack-horse roads and some have their origins in the extensive quarrying that has gone on, such as those around Loughrigg and Tilberthwaite. Numerous possibilities for mountain bike tours either of an easy or moderate grade exist. The route described samples all the different types of terrain the area has to offer and makes a good introductory ride for both beginners and experts.

Route Description

From Ambleside follow the signs for Coniston to the Rothay Bridge (narrow hump-back bridge near the Rothay Manor Hotel). Cross the bridge and turn immediately R and follow the road generally N alongside the River Rothay for 1¾m to its terminus at a bridge. Do not cross the bridge – instead turn L onto the track and follow it W as it climbs then descends to the side of Rydal Water. Continue W and follow the bridleway as it leaves Rydal Water and climbs to a low col overlooking Grasmere. At the col the bridleway forks. The L branch is Loughrigg Terrace. Follow it SW as it climbs then traverses the fellside high above Grasmere and joins the road at Red Bank. Turn L onto the road and follow it as it climbs to the Youth Hostel at High Close. Make the fine descent W towards Elterwater and take the first turning on the L after ½m (steep bend). Continue the descent then take the next L again down to the B5343. Cross straight over the B5343 and follow the road into Elterwater.

From Elterwater cross the bridge over Great Langdale Beck and follow the road S for 300yds to the start of a track on the R (easily missed). Turn R onto the track and follow it as it climbs steeply SW. The gradient soon relents and gives way to a good descent to Little Langdale road. Turn L onto the Little Langdale road and follow it E for 300yds to a lane on the R. Join the lane and follow it S to a ford and foot bridge – the ford is deceptively deep – it would take a skilled rider and dry weather to avoid wet feet! Once over the ford the track forks. Take the R branch and follow it as it climbs gradually S then SW. After ¾m the track relents and gives a fine descent to the farm at High Tilberthwaite. Go straight through the farmyard and join the road on the other side. Continue SW along the road then SE as it makes another final steep descent to join the A593. Turn R onto the A593 and follow it S for ¼m to the Low Yewdale bridleway on the L. Join the bridleway and follow it SE past Low Yewdale Farm and Boon Crag Farm to the B5285 at High Water Head. Turn L onto the B5285 and follow it as it works its way E then SE into Hawkshead.

Out of Hawkshead continue on the B5285 towards Sawrey. 250yds past the main T junction is a minor road leading to Colthouse. Turn L onto it and follow it NE to a T junction. At the junction turn L and follow the road round to the NE to a fork. Take the R branch and follow it N for 300yds to a bridleway on the R.

The bridleway climbs over Claife Heights and descends to the shores of Windermere. The first section climbs steeply S then SE. After ½m it swings NE and levels to give some pleasantly testing mountain biking. A further ¾m leads to a cross-roads. Go straight across and descend E for ¼m to another cross-roads. Again go straight across the cross-roads and head NE to make a final steep descent over the wrist shattering cobbles to the side of Windermere. Turn L onto the lakeside bridleway and follow it N to join the High Wray road after ½m. Follow the road to the T junction at High Wray. At the junction turn R and follow the road NE then NW for 1½m to the B5286. Join the B5286 and follow it N to Clappersgate. At Clappersgate turn R onto the A593 and take it NE back to Ambleside.

WALNA SCAR ROAD AND WRYNOSE PASS

N

Route --- ---
Track --- ---
Path ....

LANGDALE

ELTERWATER

YHA

Crinkle Crags

LITTLE LANGDALE

Wrynose Pass

Hardnott Pass

Wetherlam

Carrs

Grey Friar

DUNNERDALE

Tilberthwaite

YHA

YHA

Start Point
CONISTON

Dow Crag

Coniston Old Man

Walnar Scar Road

Seathwaite Bridge

Walnar Scar Pass

SEATHWAITE

Coniston Water

TORVER

A593

Caw

Walna Scar Road and Wrynose Pass

Grade: Difficult
Time: 4½ Hours
Height Gain: 2851ft
Distance: 17 Miles – 6 off road, 11 on road
Terrain: High mountain passes
Surface: Old pack-horse road with generally good going, busy road pass and old quarry tracks
Start Point Grid Reference: 303977, Coniston
Maps: O.S. The English Lakes 1:25 000 SW sheet

The Walna Scar Road which connects the Duddon Valley with Coniston has become well established as a classic mountain bike route. It crosses the high ridge of fells that extend south-west from Dow Crag, at a col between Brown Pike and Walna Scar. The Walna Scar Road was originally an old pack-horse road that linked the two communities and serviced the local quarries. This once busy route has fallen into gentle neglect, having been superceded by the opening of other routes to motor traffic. The ravages of weather and the lack of maintenance have taken a toll on the 'road', but its course can still be followed. In fact for mountain bikers its present state is perfect: plenty of tricky but rideable sections both downhill and uphill.

The longest descent can be had by following the Walna Scar Road from the Duddon Valley over to Coniston (west to east) – this gives a downhill run in excess of 3 miles. To complete the tour, use can be made of the Wrynose Pass, the Duddon Valley road and the pleasant tracks through Tilberthwaite. Although there is a lot of road work in following this route, it does have several advantages. The road down the Duddon Valley and the tracks through Tilberthwaite are particularly pleasant and the mountain scenery around Wrynose Pass is spectacular. In summer, Wrynose Pass does get very busy but watching car drivers struggle with one another and the steep hills makes for entertaining viewing!

Route Description

Out of Coniston take the A593 Ambleside road and follow it NE for 1½m to the Tilberthwaite road. Turn L onto the Tilberthwaite road and follow it NW then NE. Climb steeply at first for 1½m to the start of a track at High Tilberthwaite Farm. Go through the farm-yard and join the track. Follow it NE through woodland and old quarry workings for 1¼m to a ford and foot bridge across the River Brathy – the ford is deceptively deep! Once across the river, follow the lane on the other side N to the Little Langdale road.

Turn L onto the Little Langdale road and follow it W for 1m to a fork. The R branch leads over to Langdale. Ignore this and take the L branch which is followed as it winds its way W for 2m to the top of the pass. The road climbs from 350ft at the fork to 1270ft at the summit – a fairly stiff pull. The summit is marked by the 'Three Shire Stone', a limestone pillar which marks the spot where the old counties of Lancashire, Westmorland and Cumberland met. Continue W over Wrynose Pass and make the wonderful free-wheel down the other side. After 3¾m the road splits at Cockly Beck. The R turn is the start of Hardknott Pass. Ignore it and head SW into the Duddon Valley. Follow the Duddon Valley road for nearly 4m to a turning on the L. This turning is easily missed – look out for it as soon as you have crossed Seathwaite Bridge. Turn L and follow the narrow road as it climbs and swings E to a fork. Take the R branch and continue E along it to a gate and the start of the Walna Scar Road.

The Walna Scar Road climbs steeply SE up the rough fell by the side of Long House Gill. Follow it for ¾m to a gate in a wall. After the gate the gradient steepens further. Continue NE to a bend and follow the 'Road' around it as it eases. Traverse NE to make a final steep pull E to the top after ½m. The descent E from the top of the Walna Scar is one of the best in the district. The first section down through the zigzags is the hardest part being both steep and loose. Things ease with a long coast down to Cove Bridge until the technical difficulties of the two rock gates. Once past the rock gates, no more difficulties are encountered and a fast run down can be had, right to the centre of Coniston.

Three Shire Stone, Wrynose Pass

GRIZEDALE FOREST

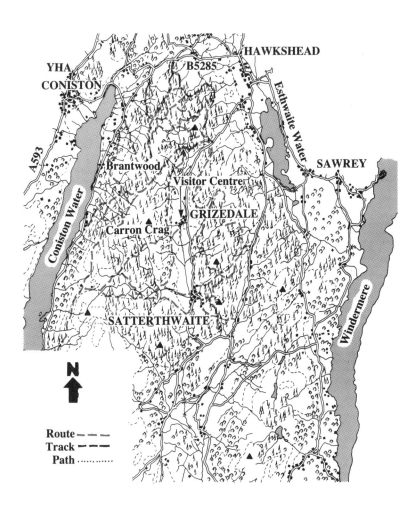

Grizedale Forest

Grade: Easy/Moderate
Time: Dependent on route chosen
Height Gain: Dependent on route chosen
Distance: 30 Miles of forest tracks and bridleways within Grizedale Forest open to mountain bikes
Terrain: Low fells and forest
Surface: Bridleways, forest tracks and roads
Start Point Grid Reference: 336944, Grizedale Forest Visitor Centre
Maps: O.S. The English Lakes 1:25 000 SE sheet, Forestry Commission map to Grizedale Forest Park

Grizedale Forest Park covers the low fells and hills east of Coniston Water and south of Hawkshead. The forest is managed by the Forestry Commission who run it primarily for the production of timber for industry. In meeting this requirement they are also able to accommodate conservation and leisure activities. Walkers, cyclists, orienteerers, art lovers and wild life enthusiasts are actively encouraged and are well catered for with accommodation, car parking, refreshments and information facilities.

The moderate terrain and the extensive network of forest roads along with existing public rights of way make Grizedale Forest Park an ideal venue for mountain bikers – particularly beginners. The Forestry Commission has recognised this and developed a series of waymarked rides. In total there are around 30 miles of mountain bike routes, including colour coded circular routes, other forest roads open to bicycles and bridleways. These tours can be used for short circular tours taking no more than an hour or longer tours lasting all day. Route finding is best done with the aid of the Forestry Commission's own Grizedale Forest Park Map available at the visitor centre for a modest sum. It clearly details all route options and is drawn at a large scale (3 inches to 1 mile).

Most activities are centred around the Visitor Centre which is well signposted and can be reached from Hawkshead in the north and from Newby Bridge via Satterthwaite in the south.

Warning

Grizedale Forest Park is being actively worked. At all times keep clear of tree felling, do not approach working machinery and observe warning signs. Also, please observe 'no cycling' signs and do not cycle on footpaths or waymarked walks. Do remember the roads are used by Forestry Commission Vehicles and have care for yourself and others.

Green Moor

WOODLAND

Woodland Fell

White Borran

Cockenskell

Yeat House

Appletree Holme

Blawith Knott

Tottlebank

Start Point

BLAWITH

Subberthwaite Common

Kiln Bank

Raisthwaite Lane

Birch Bank

Cat Nest

Little Burney

Great Burney

N

Route — — —
Track ━ ━ ━
Path ·············

Subberthwaite Common

Grade: Easy
Time: 1½ Hours
Height Gain: 550ft
Distance: 7½ Miles – 4 off road, 3½ on road
Terrain: Low fells
Surface: Quiet roads, boggy tracks and rough lanes
Start Point Grid Reference: 288883, Blawith
Maps: O.S. Pathfinder, Broughton in Furness and Newby Bridge, SD 28/38. Landranger 96, 1:50 000

Subberthwaite Common and the Blawith Fells lie at the south-west tip of Coniston Water. Most people tend to ignore this quiet corner of Lakeland and speed on by to the greater heights of the nearby Coniston Fells. This is a pity as this attractive area of low fells and moorland is laced with interesting bridleways.

The modest heights encountered in these parts make for more leisurely mountain biking – the greatest altitude reached on a bridleway is 525ft on the side of Woodland Fell. Nevertheless, plenty of entertaining riding can be had, particularly the lane to Kiln Bank and the descent across the side of Woodland Fell.

Route Description

From the A5084 at Blawith take the minor road opposite the church and follow it W for ½m to a junction. Take the R fork (metalled) and follow it N then W for another ½m until a private road at Appletree Holme. Do not take the private road: continue past it for a few yards to the start of a bridleway on the L, around the back of the rock outcrop. Take the bridleway and follow it W as it climbs to join a lane, which then leads to a ford. After the ford the bridleway breaks out onto open fellside. It should be followed as it climbs first W then NW for ½m to round a low col overlooking the Woodland Valley. From the col the bridleway swings W and gives a good descent through a couple of bends and then by a beck to a bridge at Green Moor. Ignore the bridge and take the rough bridleway that climbs S for ½m after which it levels and then descends to the SW (metalled) to join a road.

At the road turn R and follow it for a short distance to a junction. Go straight

across the junction (L) and follow the road S for 1m to another junction. Take the L fork as it climbs steeply E around a long bend to the start of a bridleway at a sharp bend ($\frac{1}{3}$m). Continue E along the bridleway to a junction on Subberthwaite Common. Take the road NE to Birch Bank. From Birch Bank follow the bridleway around the back of the farm and head E across pasture and join the lane to Kiln Bank. At Kiln Bank follow the bridleway past the farm buildings and join Long Lane, which after $\frac{1}{4}$m joins Raisthwaite Lane at a crossroads. Turn L and follow Raisthwaite Lane NE for 1m back to Blawith.

DEVOKE WATER AND ULPHA FELL

ESKDALE GREEN

Devoke Water

Raven Crag

Birkby Fell

Barnscar

Woodend

Woodend Height

Dyke

BROAD OAK

Hesk Fell▲

▲Stainton Pike

ULPHA

WABERTHWAITE

Start Point

Whitfell▲

Burn Moor▲

Bigert Mire

N

Buck Barrow

River Duddon

Route — — —
Track — — —
Path ···········

Corney Fell

A595

DUDDON BRIDGE

Devoke Water and Ulpha Fell

Grade: Difficult
Time: 5 Hours
Height Gain: 2035ft
Distance: 14½ Miles – 6½ off road, 8 on road
Terrain: High coastal fells
Surface: Fell and valley roads, access tracks, vague bridleways over heather moorland and grassy fellside
Start Point Grid Reference: 198936, Ulpha
Maps: O.S. The English Lakes 1:25 000 SW sheet, O.S. Landranger 96 1:50 000

Devoke Waters, Lakeland's biggest tarn, is unusual in that it has wide, almost totally unrestricted views. Most other tarns are usually tucked away at the backs of corries or hidden amongst trees. Even Burnmoor Tarn, its closest rival cannot compete with Devoke Water's panoramic views.

Set amongst the modest coastal peaks south of Eskdale, Devoke Water is passed by a surprisingly challenging bridleway. Although this bridleway does not gain a great altitude the terrain it crosses can prove quite tricky. Its course on the ground is not always clear, particularly amongst the wet heather moorland of Birkby Fell – navigational skills will be well tested here in poor visibility.

To complete a mountain bike tour, the bridleway crossing the flanks of Whitfell, which lies 2½ miles to the south of Devoke Water, provides a higher altitude, but less demanding return leg.

Route Description

From Ulpha take the Ulpha Fell road which climbs steeply NW. Follow it for 3½m to a crossroads. Turn L and follow the Devoke Water access track SW for 1m to a fork just after a ford. Take the R branch and follow the bridleway as it skirts W along the shores of Devoke Water. Once past the W end of Devoke Water the bridleway climbs slightly to a low col. Follow the bridleway NW a short distance as it descends past some ancient cairns. Past the cairns the bridleway becomes vague. It swings round to the SW and is followed as it descends generally in this direction for 1½m to a gate in the corner of an intake wall. Stay on the N side of Black Beck – a very wet section. Go through the gate

101

and continue W along the bridleway as it descends then climbs slightly to the start of a lane after ½m. Turn L and follow the lane S then SW to a gate. At the gate take the track that winds its way W to the farm at Dyke. Go through the farmyard and join the A595.

Turn L onto the A595 and follow it S for ½m to a junction. At the junction turn L onto the Corney Fell road. Follow the Corney Fell road SE for ½m as it climbs to a turning – Fell Lane. Turn L onto Fell Lane and follow it E to a bend. A bridleway starts at the bend. Join the bridleway and follow it as it climbs E for 2½m. The first section along the N side of Whitrow Beck climbs moderately. After the beck is crossed the gradient soon steepens across Waberthwaite Fell and only relents as the col NW of Whitfell is reached.

From the col the bridleway works its way generally SE for 1½m giving a fast descent over grassy fellside to the farm at Bigert Mire. Go through the farmyard and follow the lane S then E then S again to join the minor road. Turn L onto the minor road and follow it as it descends E then NE for 1¼m to the junction at Ulpha Bridge. Join the Duddon Valley road and follow it NE back to Ulpha.

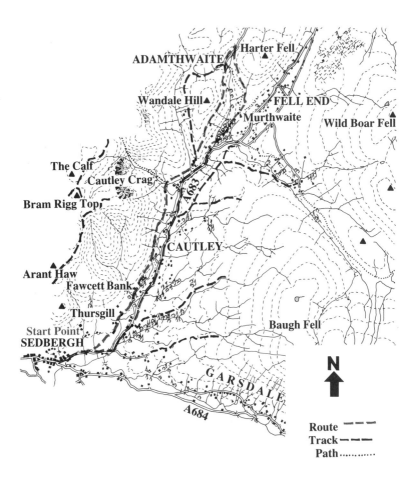

Cautley and Wandale

Grade: Moderate
Time: 2-2½ Hours
Height Gain: 1062ft
Distance: 14 Miles – 7 off road, 7 on road
Terrain: Valleys and rounded fells
Surface: Busy valley road, farm tracks, steep wooded bridleway and well-graded grassy bridleways
Start Point Grid Reference: 659922, Sedbergh
Maps: O.S. Pathfinder 617 1:25 000, O.S. Landranger 91 & 98 1:50 000

The Howgill Fells are separated from the Lake District and the Yorkshire Dales by the River Lune and the River Rawthey. The Lune starts its life heading north then does a complete loop around the Howgills to form the eastern, northern and western boundaries, finally draining south towards Lancaster and Morecambe Bay. The eastern and southern boundaries are completed by the Rawthey which flows south-west into the Lune at Killington to the south of Sedbergh.

The course of the River Rawthey is followed closely by two routes. The A683 crosses it from Sedbergh then follows its eastern side over its watershed to head north-east to Kirkby Stephen. On its western side is an old bridleway which links the farms at Adamthwaite and Narthwaith with those at Cautley and Sedbergh.

In descent the bridleway makes an excellent mountain bike ride and allows views towards the impressive waterfall, Cautley Spout, which tumbles in steps over Cautley Crag. To reach the start at Adamthwaite it is best to take the A684 and then a bridleway past Murthwaite. The bridleway up to Murthwaite is the crux of this tour being steep and amongst dense woodland more reminiscent of jungle warfare – but persist, the riding after it is well worth it.

Route Description

From Sedbergh take the A684 and follow it E then NE for 5m until it is possible to turn R onto a track over Handley's Bridge. Cross the bridge and follow the track a short distance to a T junction. Turn R and follow the track NE as it descends to a ford. Cross the ford and continue NE, climbing up through the dense woodland. There are numerous pony tracks through the trees. Try to stay as near the ridge line as possible. After 300yds the trees give way to pasture. Continue NE up the broad ridge line for a further ½m to the farm at Murthwaite. Past the farm continue NE for 250yds, ignoring the paths on the R, to a fork. Take the L branch and follow it N as it climbs easily for ½m to another fork. Take the L branch and follow the excellent track as it climbs

then descends N to the Adamthwaite road after ¾m.

Join the Adamthwaite road and follow it SW for ½m to its terminus at Adamthwaite Farm and the start of a bridleway. The bridleway passes through the lower yard on the E side of the farm. Once through the yard join the lane and follow it as it climbs slightly then descends S then SW for 2m to the farm at Narthwaite – the last section down to Narthwaite is along an old lane with collapsed walls and can prove a little tricky. The bridleway splits at Narthwaite farm. Take the R fork which leads W then NW down to a ford. Turn L over the ford and follow the bridleway S then SW for ¾m to a ford and foot bridge over Cautley Home Beck – do not cross the ford through the River Rawthey. Once over the beck follow the bridleway as it skirts the fellside and heads SW through pasture for 2m to Fawcett Bank. Past Fawcett Bank join the good track and continue SW along it for ½m to the road at Thursgill. Join the road and follow it SW back to the A683. Turn R onto the A683 and take it back to Sedbergh.

Fawcett Bank

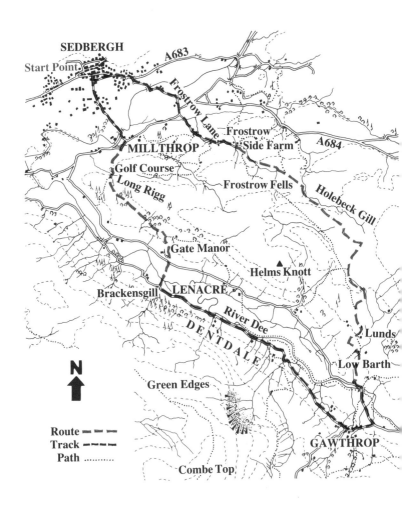

SEDBERGH

Start Point

A683

Frostrow Lane

Frostrow
Side Farm

A684

MILLTHROP

Golf Course

Long Rigg

Frostrow Fells

Holebeck Gill

Gate Manor

Helms Knott

Brackensgill

LENACRE

River Dee

DENTDALE

Lunds

Low Barth

N

Green Edges

Combe Top

GAWTHROP

Route - - -
Track - - - -
Path ....

Frostrow Fells and Dentdale

Grade: Easy
Time: 2 Hours
Height Gain: 908ft
Distance: 8 Miles – 4 on road, 4 off road
Terrain: Valleys and low fells
Surface: Roads, stony access tracks, grassy bridleways and narrow lanes
Start Point Grid Reference: 660922, Sedbergh
Maps: O.S. Yorkshire Dales 1:25 000 Western Area (just!), O.S. Landranger 97 & 98 1:50 000

Of all the Yorkshire Dales, Dentdale has probably the most pleasant atmosphere. With a westerly aspect it receives the sun for most of the day making it more verdant and giving it a softer feel than some of its more dour neighbours. None of Dentdale's fells are more pleasant than the Frostrow Fells. This little area of rolling fells lies on the north side of Dentdale and to the south of Sedbergh. Each side of the Frostrow Fells has numerous small hamlets and farms which are interlinked by narrow lanes and bridleways. Two of these rights of way cross over the fells from north to south and can be followed on mountain bikes to give a tour with no real technical difficulties or navigational problems.

Route Description

Out of Sedbergh take the Dentdale road to the S then SE for ½m to the bridge over the River Rawthey. Cross the bridge and follow the road round to the Millthrop turning. Turn L and follow it to a T junction in the village. Turn R and take the road SW through Millthrop a short distance to a bridleway on the L. This is the Frostrow Golf Club track. Ascend SW along it then S past the club house (old hut!) to a ford. Cross the ford and take the track on the other side SW then S to a gate. Go through the gate and take the grassy bridleway as it winds its way SE across pasture to a lane. Continue SE along the lane which gives a good run down towards Dentdale. After ½m the bridleway forks. Take the L fork and continue along the lane to another fork. This time take the R fork and follow it by the high garden wall to the Dentdale road.

The route now joins the bridleway down the narrow lane opposite, but this involves crossing a deep ford: if the river is in spate or you do not fancy getting your feet wet, then turn L and follow the main Dentdale road SE for 2m to a lane 125yds before Barth Bridge (not the footpath right by the bridge); if the river is not in spate then cross the deep ford and take the track up the other side to the road. Turn L onto the road and follow it SE down Dentdale for 2m to Gawthrop. Follow the road E through Gawthrop to a T junction on the main

Only in a very dry summer will you get across the ford with dry feet.

Dentdale road. Turn L and follow the road back NW to the start of a lane 125yds past Barth Bridge.

The lane zigzags N up the fellside for ¾m to its terminus in front of the farm at Lunds. Take it to Lunds – ignoring all the farm entrances (this is obvious on the ground). A bridleway starts on the L (W) side of the farm at Lunds between the house and the barn. Take it and join the lane which winds its way N up the fellside for ½m to a fork by a sheep pen. Take the L branch through by the sheep pen and follow it NW then N along the wall for ½m to a wall on a low col. This is the start of the descent back down to Sedbergh. Go through the gate and follow the bridleway NE alongside the wall. After ¼m the bridleway leaves the wall and descends over open moorland. Its course is vague in parts, but generally it continues NE until it reaches a ford after 1m. Cross the ford and join the narrow lane on the other side. This is Frostrow Lane which is followed down for ½m to a fork. Take the R branch to another fork. This time take the L branch and take it down to the A684. Turn L onto the A684 and follow it W back over the River Rawthey to its junction with the A683. Then take the A684 W back to Sedbergh.

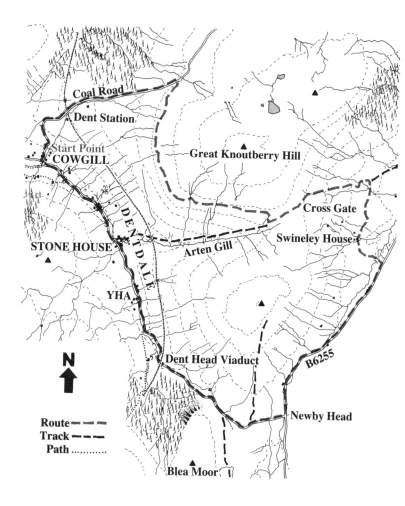

The Flanks of Great Knoutberry Hill

Grade: Moderate
Time: 2 Hours
Height Gain: 1171ft
Distance: 10½ Miles – 4 off road, 6½ on road
Terrain: Valley and exposed moorland
Surface: Narrow valley roads, farm tracks and grassy lane
Start Point Grid Reference: 761869, Cowgill
Maps: O.S. Yorkshire Dales 1:25 000 Western Area, Landranger 98 1:50 000

The old pack-horse road on the slopes of Great Knoutberry Hill, high above Dentdale, follows a superb, if illogical, course. It seems to go nowhere and serve no purpose. Originally, however, it serviced the small collieries and marble quarries in Arten Gill which have long since ceased and left this grassy lane blissfully quiet. The problem though is reaching the pack-horse road. Gaining each end either from Dent Station or Widdale Head involves a fairly stiff climb – amply rewarded, however, by excellent riding and expansive views.

Route Description

From the bridge over the River Dee at Cowgill, take the Dentdale valley road, and follow it SE for 3½m to a T junction. The first 2m are relatively easy; after which the road starts to climb steeply and makes the long haul to a high point at Newby Head Gate – passing under the Dent Head Viaduct which carries the Settle to Carlisle railway line. A short descent from Newby Head Gate then leads to the junction.

From the T junction turn L onto the B6255 Hawes road and follow it as it descends NE for 1½m to the start of a bridleway on the L. The bridleway leads past Swineley House. Take it and follow it over Widdale Beck and on up to the farm-yard at Swineley House. The bridleway heads NE through 2 gates and then alongside the wall – vague at first. After the wall the bridleway heads N for ½m across rough pasture and climbs to join a track after fording Lings Beck. This track climbs steadily W to the head of Arten Gill. Follow it to the col and then as it descends towards Arten Gill. Before it reaches Arten Gill, however, a lane branches off to the R. This is the start of the pack-horse road. Take it and follow it as it climbs N then levels to swing round to the W. Continue easily W then N as it traverses the flanks of Great Knoutberry Hill for 2m to the Coal Road. Turn L onto the Coal Road and follow it as it descends steeply W past Dent Station to Cowgill – a fast descent with a couple of hairpins to finish!

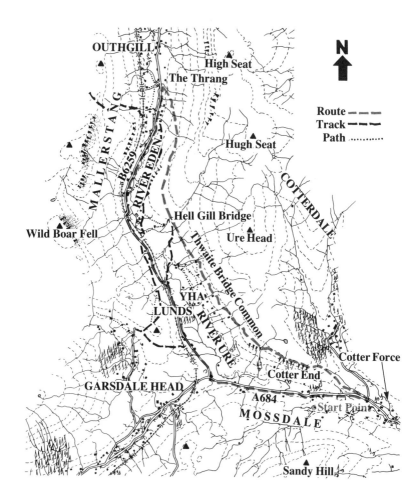

Lady Ann Clifford Highway

Grade: Difficult
Time: 3½ Hours
Height Gain: 1345ft
Distance: 15 Miles – 7½ off road, 7½ on road
Terrain: Valley and high moorland
Surface: Boggy and steep bridleways, stone moorland tracks and roads
Start Point Grid Reference: 842921, A684 Cotterdale turning, Landranger 98
Maps: O.S. Landranger 91 & 98 1:50 000

The Eden and Ure watershed provides a breach in the hills on the northern boundary of the Yorkshire Dales National Park, at the head of Wensleydale. This breach is exploited by the Settle to Carlisle Railway Line and the B6259 Garsdale Head to Kirkby Stephen road. Both of these routes cross the watershed at its lowest point. Taking a higher and more adventurous route is the Lady Ann Clifford Highway, a former drove road. This bridleway was used by Lady Ann Clifford as she commuted between her estates in the 16th century.

Although there is little in it, the longest downhill run on a mountain bike can be had along the Lady Ann Clifford Highway by following it south to north. This means tackling the steep ascent up the sweeping, grassy ridge of Cotter End first. Once this is completed, the going becomes interesting with numerous, technically entertaining sections through some fine moorland scenery.

Two thirds along the highway is Hell Gill Bridge which spans a deep, narrow gorge and forms the National Park boundary. Heading south from the bridge is a bridleway back to the B6259. This can be used to shorten the route considerably – a good alternative if you tire or the weather deteriorates.

Route Description

From the Cotterdale junction on the A684 take the Lady Ann Clifford Highway NW up the broad grassy ridge (signposted). It gradually steepens until a wall is reached after 1m. Pass through the gate in the wall and follow the bridleway as it zigzags W past the old kiln to finally level out on top of Cotter End. From Cotter End the bridleway skirts W then NW along the edge of Thwaite Bridge Common for 2m to some old farm buildings at High Dyke.

115

Continue NW past High Dyke as the bridleway descends slowly and becomes more technical. After 1½m the old farm at Washer Gill is reached. Follow the bridleway across the picturesque ford and take the lower track as it skirts round the fellside to head NW again. Past Washer Gill the going eases and the bridleway descends slightly to Hell Gill Bridge after ½m.

If you want to shorten the route take the vague bridleway S from Hell Gill Bridge to join the B6259. Otherwise, cross the bridge and continue NW as the bridleway climbs for 1m then swings N. Continue across the rise and then follow the bridleway as it descends N for 2m across the flanks of The Thrang to join the B6259. Turn L onto the B6259 and follow it S for 2½m as it climbs back up onto the watershed. Continue over the top and follow the B6259 as it descends SW for 2½m to the A684 at Garsdale Head. Turn L onto the A684 and follow it E for 2½m back to the Cotterdale turning.

Old lime kiln on Cotter End.

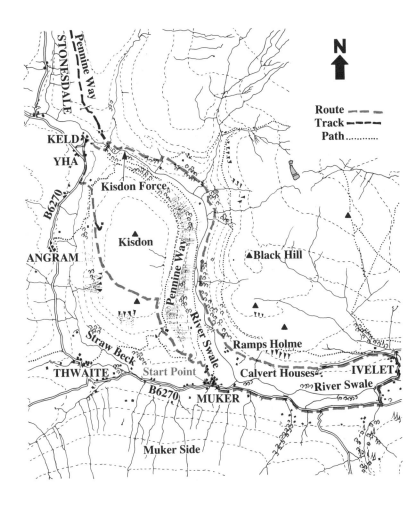

N

Route — — —
Track ━ ━ ━
Path ....

STONESDALE
Pennine Way
KELD
YHA
B6270
Kisdon Force
Kisdon
ANGRAM
Pennine Way
River Swale
Black Hill
Straw Beck
Ramps Holme
THWAITE
Start Point
Calvert Houses
IVELET
B6270
MUKER
River Swale
Muker Side

Kisdon

Grade: Difficult
Time: 2½ Hours
Height Gain: 1530ft
Distance: 9 Miles – 6 off road, 3 on road
Terrain: Limestone fell and valleys
Surface: Steep bridleway, exposed fell top, farm tracks and roads
Start Point Grid Reference: 910979, Muker Landranger 98
Maps: O.S. Yorkshire Dales 1:25 000 Northern Area, Landranger 91 & 98 1:50 000

Kisdon sits like an island amongst the surrounding hills at the head of Swaledale. This little peak divides the infant Swale from its other main tributary Straw Beck. The eastern side forms an impressively steep side gorge through which the Swale flows. On the western side the ground is nearly as precipitous with limestone crags falling away towards Angram.

Two routes cross Kisdon's flanks but neither actually reach its summit. The 'Pennine Way' skirts the eastern side whilst a bridleway crosses its southern ridge then skirts along the top of its western crags. A short but challenging mountain bike ride can be had by ascending this bridleway direct from Muker then following it over Kisdon to join a bridleway back along the River Swale from Keld.

Route Description

From Muker join the lane (bridleway) at the back of the village and follow it for 250yds NW then N to a junction. Turn L and follow the steep track as it zigzags NW for ¾m into a lane then to a fork. Take the R branch and follow it N to a bend. Continue on the track as it swings W then NW to a broad col. This is the highest point reached in Kisdon by the bridleway – the summit lies ½m to the N.

From the col descend NW passing the old mine workings and follow the bridleway as it swings to the N giving a good run down to join an access track after ¾m. Follow the track as it descends N then W to make a final short climb to join the Keld road. Turn R onto the Keld road and follow it NE for ¼m to a lane on the R. Make the turning and follow the lane down into Keld village. Just behind the church in Keld is the start of a bridleway. Join it and follow it NE a

short distance to a fork. Take the L branch and follow it to a bridge over the River Swale. Cross the bridge and follow the bridleway up the other bank to join the Stonesdale bridleway.

Turn R onto the bridleway and follow the track over East Gill and up the hill on the other side. Just round the corner is Kisdon Force, an impressive waterfall that is easily reached by a short walk. From Kisdon Force follow the track SW then S through the huge gorge formed by the River Swale to Ramps Holme Farm. Continue along a rocky terrace for the first 1m. The track then drops down to the valley floor. From Ramps Holme Farm continue a short distance along the track to a junction. Take the L fork and follow it W to join a road which leads in 1½m down into Ivelet. From Ivelet back-track E and cross the River Swale to join the B6270. Turn R and follow it for 1½m back to Muker.

Fasten all gates

Kisdon and Swaledale from East Stonesdale Farm

121

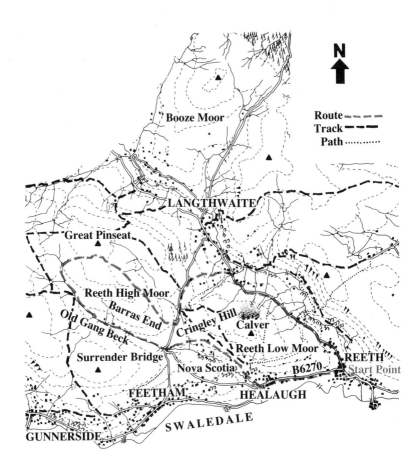

Reeth Moors

Grade: Easy
Time: 3½ Hours
Height Gain: 1335ft
Distance: 12 Miles – 8 off road, 4 on road
Terrain: Valleys and high moorland
Surface: Valley roads, stony lane, grassy bridleways and old mining tracks
Start Point Grid Reference: 038994, Reeth, Landranger 98
Maps: O.S. Yorkshire Dales 1:25 000 Northern and Central Area, Landranger 91 & 98 1:50 000

Reeth Moors, on the north side of Swaledale, have been extensively mined for lead. The abandoned workings and extensive gravel tips have left parts of the moors looking more like the surface of the moon, whilst other parts remain unscathed and still retain their natural look. The old tracks which used to service these mines are mostly still intact and have been adopted as bridleways. They provide easy mountain biking through this contrasting and almost surreal landscape.

The most obvious mountain bike route is the bridleway that does a loop around Reeth High Moor, up alongside Old Gang Beck, and then passes close by the summit of Great Pinseat finally descending Barras End. This loop can easily be extended by making use of the bridleways on the north and south sides of Reeth Low Moor, giving a total tour of 12 miles from Reeth.

Route Description

From Reeth take the B6270 W for 1½m to Healaugh. Continue through Healaugh to a fork. Turn R off the B6270 and head W up the road for 225yds to a lane. Turn R onto the lane and follow it NW for ½m to woodland – ignore the turning on the R. Continue NW through the woodland. On the other side the bridleway zigzags NW up the fellside. Follow it alongside the wall then W across open fell. The bridleway then descends back alongside a wall to a beck after 1¼m. Cross the beck and follow the bridleway W for ½m to the road. Turn L and follow the road a short distance down to a track at the side of Surrender Bridge.

This is the Old Gang Smelting Mills track which follows the course of Old Gang Beck. Join it and follow it as it climbs easily NW for 2m to a fork at Level House Bridge. Take the R branch and continue NW along for ¾m to a ford. Cross the ford and follow the track as it heads E up the gravel beds and tips of

Forefield Rake for ³⁄₄m to a broad col just S of Great Pinseat (numerous cairns).

The col marks the high point of the route. From it the track swings SE first across grass, then a short boggy section which soon gives way to a good stony track. Follow it for 2m as it gradually steepens to give a good run down to the road. Turn L onto the road and take it N for ¼m across a ford and then up a short rise to the start of a bridleway on the R. This bridleway skirts the N side of Reeth Low Moor. Join it and make the short climb to a fork. Take the L branch and follow it to another fork. Take the L branch again and head E then NE along it as it descends across open moorland for 1½m down to the Arkengarthdale road. Turn R onto the road and head SE along it back to Reeth.

Trig point, Great Pinseat

Unusual cairn on the south side of Great Pinseat

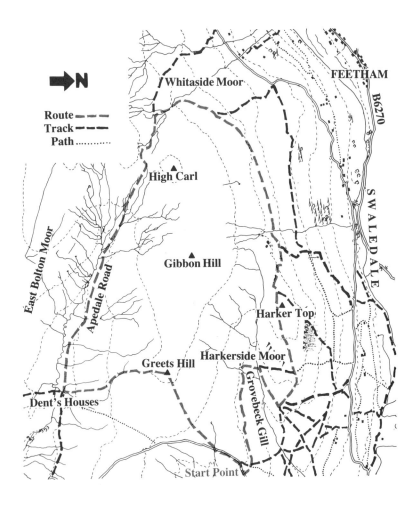

Apedale and Greets Hill

Grade: Moderate
Time: 2½-3 Hours
Height Gain: 1144ft
Distance: 9½ Miles – 9 off road, ½ on road
Terrain: Moorland and low fells
Surface: Fell road, stony access tracks and grassy bridleway
Start Point Grid Reference: 042967, Grinton Moor road, Landranger 98
Maps: O.S. Yorkshire Dales 1:25 000 Central and Northern Area, Landranger 98 1:50 000

Apedale is separated from Swaledale by a ridge of three tops: High Carl at the western end, Gibbon Hill in the centre and Greets Hill at the eastern end. This ridge is crossed by a bridleway at Greets Hill which forms an excellent link for a mountain bike ride along the Apedale road and then across Harkerside Moor on the old mining tracks.

All the tracks and bridleways around this ridge are still in reasonable repair and give good riding. Particularly fine is the descent from Greets Hill south to Dent's Houses at the start of the Apedale road which, if followed means a clockwise circuit of this tour – though once completed you will probably want to go round again in the opposite direction!

Route Description

From the layby at the start of the Grovebeck bridleway, take the Grinton Fell road as it climbs SW for ½m to the start of a bridleway at a culvert over Ridley Hush. Turn R onto the bridleway and follow it as it heads SW for ¾m to Greets Hill. The bridleway is a little vague at first but soon becomes clearer on the S side of the mine washings. From Greets Hill a good track heads S. Take it and follow it down for 1m to the crossroads near Dent's Houses – this is the start of the Apedale road.

Turn R onto the Apedale road as it heads W. For the first 1½m the Apedale road climbs steadily and gradually, swinging round to the NW. It then steepens for a final ¾m and turns SW onto a broad col below High Carl. From the col follow the bridleway through the gate, past the big hole and descend N then W along it for ½m to a fork. Take the R branch alongside the shooting butts. Follow it as it descends and skirts the flanks of High Carl, first N then NE and

127

finally E for 2½m to the track on Harker Top – ignore the bridleways and paths which descend towards Swaledale. Past Harker Top continue E on the track and follow it along the ridge. The track drops over the end of the ridge and descends SE to a fork. Ignore the L branch and continue SE to a T junction. Turn R and follow the shooting track SW. The track skirts around the head of Grovebeck Gill to finally head E and is followed back for 1½m to the Grinton Moor road.

Dent's Houses

ARKENGARTHDALE AND MORESDALE ROAD

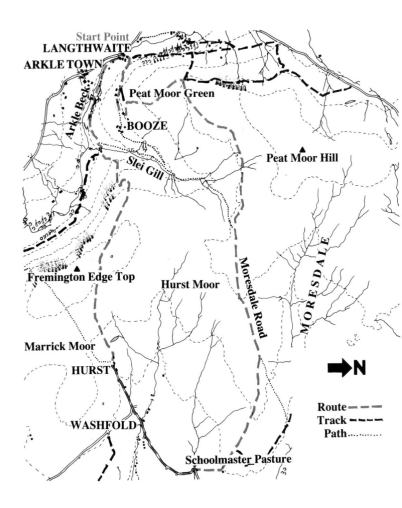

Start Point
LANGTHWAITE
ARKLE TOWN

Arkle Beck

Peat Moor Green

BOOZE

Slei Gill

Peat Moor Hill

Fremington Edge Top

Hurst Moor

Moresdale Road

MORESDALE

Marrick Moor

HURST

N

WASHFOLD

Schoolmaster Pasture

Route
Track
Path

Arkengarthdale and Moresdale Road

Grade: Moderate
Time: 2½-3 Hours
Height Gain: 1495ft
Distance: 9½ Miles – 8 off road, 1½ on road
Terrain: High moorland
Surface: Steep bridleway, stony shooting tracks, narrow roads and steep grassy bridleway
Start Point Grid Reference: 005025, Langthwaite, Landranger 92
Maps: O.S. Yorkshire Dales 1:25 000 Central and Northern Area, O.S. Landranger 92 1:50 000

Arkengarthdale is the most northerly dale in the Yorkshire Dales National Park. The moors on the north-east side of this off-shoot from Swaledale are crossed by the National Park's boundary, which is roughly aligned to the watershed. Across the boundary and the watershed on these high, windswept moors are two routes. To the north is the Moresdale road and the old link between Booze in Arkengarthdale and Moresdale – now maintained as a shooting track. To the south is a bridleway which follows a line of old mine and quarry workings over Fremington Edge.

Moresdale Road and the Fremington Edge bridleway give excellent mountain biking and are easy to follow. The Arkengarthdale side of both routes tends to be quite steep whilst the Moresdale and Hurst side tends to fall away more gently. To take advantage of the differing gradients it is best to start at Langthwaite on the Arkengarthdale side and follow the Mosedale Road east, thus gaining height quickly and making the most of the long run down the Mosedale side. The return leg is via the easy ascent through Hurst and along the bridleway to Fremington Edge, finishing with a superb descent into Slei Gill.

Route Description

From Langthwaite take the steep, narrow road as it climbs N then E to Booze. In Booze the road forks into 2 tracks. Take the L branch which climbs NE towards a farm. Just before the farm the track turns through a hairpin bend beside an abandoned building. Head W up it to another bend. Follow the track N around the bend and then alongside the wall to a gate. Go through the gate

the shooting track N for 300yds to a fork. Then take the R branch which is followed NE then E to rejoin the Moresdale road after ¾m.

Once rejoined, the Moresdale road is then followed as it climbs easily E for 1m to the National Park boundary at Stony Man – ignoring the track on the L above the shooting hut. Stony Man is a stone boundary post – from it the Moresdale road starts to descend. Continue E along it, ignoring all the tracks on the L, for 2m to the farm at Schoolmaster Pasture. In front of the farm turn R and follow the track down to a bridge and the start of a road (Goat Road). Join the road and follow it SW through Washfold for 1½m to Hurst.

From Hurst a bridleway heads W to Fremington Edge. Join it as it climbs through old mine workings for just under 1m to a vague fork marked by a cairn. Take the L branch W across grass and heather for 350yds to a gap in the corner of a wall. Through the gap the bridleway crosses grass NE to a group of cairns. From the cairns continue NE and make the superb descent which winds its way over smooth grass, along a terrace, over more smooth grass and finally along a steep lane to the Storthwaite Hall farm. From Storthwaite Hall take the bridleway that heads W. Follow it over the ford and up the short climb. It then descends through woodland and leads back to Langthwaite alongside Arkle Beck.

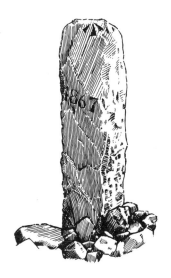

Stony Man, Boundary Mark

Start of the descent into Arkengarthdale from Fremington Edge top

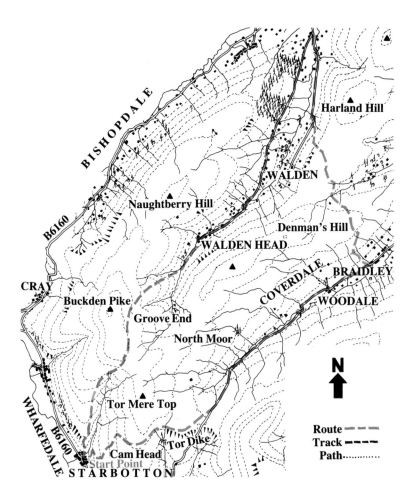

Route ‑ ‑ ‑
Track ▬ ▬ ▬
Path ....

Buckden Pike and Top Mere

Grade: Very Difficult
Time: 5 Hours
Height Gain: 2903ft
Distance: 20 Miles – 11 off road, 9 on road
Terrain: Valleys and high fells
Surface: Steep fell tracks, boggy bridleways and narrow roads
Start Point Grid Reference: 953749, Starbotton
Maps: O.S. Yorkshire Dales 1:25 000 Central Area, Landranger 98
1:50 000

Buckden Pike is one of the few major peaks in the Yorkshire Dales which has routes to it open to mountain bikers. One goes straight to the summit trig point whilst another crosses its southern ridge. The southern bridleway starts at Starbotton in Wharfedale and crosses over to Walden. It gives high level riding over rounded grassy fells. Further south again, along the ridge from Buckden Pike is another bridleway which crosses the flanks of the subsidiary peak, Tor Mere Top. The descent into Wharfedale via this bridleway is particularly exciting – along the steep and winding Starbotton Cam road.

To link the two southern routes over the Buckden Pike ridge, a bridleway from Walden to Braidley over the boggy Braidley Moor can be taken. This completes a tour that should not be undertaken lightly, for although the technical difficulties are limited, the terrain is arduous and can be quite tricky to cross under poor weather conditions.

Route Description

Take the steep track that zigzags N out of Starbotton on the W side of Cam Gill Beck. The first section up the lane is steep but it soon relents a little to lead 1m to a fork. Take the R branch and follow it N then E for ½m to another fork. This time take the L branch (main track) and take it NE as it steepens and climbs to a boundary stone on the Buckden Pike ridge. From the boundary stone take the bridleway N as it skirts the flank of Buckden Pike. After ¾m the bridleway swings round to the NE and is followed as it descends Walden Moor for 1¼m to a confluence of two becks. Cross the ford and continue NE along the bridleway on the SE side of Walden Beck to the road at Walden Head.

The road descends NE along Walden. Take it for 4m to a junction. Turn R and back-track S along it on the other side of Walden for 1½m as the road climbs to the start of a bridleway. Turn L onto the bridleway and ascend the grassy track S then SE for ½m until it splits. Take the L fork and continue SE

along it to another fork. Take the R branch around the gill to a ford. Cross the ford and head SE ignoring the track on the L for ¼m to a further fork. Turn R onto the bridleway as it climbs S to the top of a short rise. Follow the bridleway over the rise then make the steep descent S along it to Braidley in Coverdale.

At Braidley join the valley road and take it SW as it climbs for 4m to the start of the Top Mere bridleway. Join the bridleway and follow it SW across open moorland then W along the top of Tor Dike to join the Starbotton Cam road after 1¼m. Join the Starbotton Cam road and follow the bridleway SW along it for ¼m to a fork. Take the R branch and head SW along it as it skirts the S ridge of Top Mere to a walled lane. Join the lane and make the excellent descent along it back to Starbotton.

Boundary stone on the flanks of Buckden Pike.

Head north from Buckden Pike across Walden Moor

Embsay Moor

Grade: Easy
Time: 4-4½ Hours
Height Gain: 2017ft
Distance: 20½ Miles – 10¾ off road, 9¾ on road
Terrain: Valley and exposed moorland
Surface: Grassy bridleway, shooting tracks and roads
Start Point Grid Reference: 073542, Bolton Abbey
Maps: O.S. Yorkshire Dales 1:25 000 Southern Area

Embsay and Barden, on the west side of Wharfedale between Skipton and Grassington have been opened up to public access, under an agreement between Yorkshire Dales National Park and the landowners. Unfortunately this agreement was reached prior to the growth of mountain biking and no provision was made for bicycles. The only legally rideable route across the splendidly wild moors is along the bridleway which stretches east to west linking Bolton Abbey with Rylstone.

The bridleway probably has monastic origins connecting Bolton Abbey with its Wharfedale and Malham estates. Now though, most of its course is aligned to shooting tracks which are generally well kept and provide easy riding. The only section which may force you out of the saddle is the ascent to Westy Bank Wood and onto Middle Hare Head. To return, sections of the Yorkshire Dales Cycle Route give pleasant riding back to join the bridleway at Hare Head, which then gives an excellent descent back to Bolton Abbey.

Route Description

The bridleway starts on the W side of the B6160 at Bolton Hall. Take it NW as it climbs a track then pasture and passes by a pond to Westy Bank Wood. Follow the bridleway as it zigzags NW through the wood. On the other side continue NW then W for 1½m to the shallow col on the S side of Middle Hare Head. Over the col descend W for ½m to a road. Turn L onto the road and follow it for 250yds as it climbs S to the start of a bridleway. Join the bridleway and follow it easily NW for 1m to a fork. Take the R branch N 200yds to another fork. Take the L fork as it climbs NW for 1⅓m to a broad col at Brown Bank.

The col is the start of the main descent. Head W on the bridleway for ½m to

Gate at High Hare Head.

a fork. Take the R branch which then skirts W around the head of Waterfall Gill for 1m to a small rise on Sun Moor Hill. From Sun Moor Hill the bridleway steepens considerably to give a good descent NW for ³/₄m to join a lane. Turn R onto the lane and take it N to join the B6265. Turn R and follow the B6265 into Rylstone.

From Rylstone continue N on the B6265 through Cracoe for 1¹/₂m to a fork on a bend. Turn R onto Thorpe Lane and follow it as it climbs NE for 2¹/₂m to a T junction. Turn R and follow the road SW into Thorpe then NE out of it for ¹/₂m to join the B6160. Turn R and head SE along the B6160 on the W side of the River Wharfe for 4¹/₂m to the Embsay road. Turn R and follow the Embsay road SW as it climbs for 1¹/₄m to the Bolton Abbey bridleway at Hare Head. Turn L onto the bridleway and retrace it E over Middle Hare Head and back down to Bolton Abbey.

N

Route — — —
Track — — —
Path ....

Proctor High Mark

KILNSEY

W H A R F E D A L E

Holegates

Mastiles Gate

Mastiles Lane

B6160

Malham Cove

Gordale Scar

Bordley

Threshfield Moor

THRESHFIELD

The Weets

MALHAM

Moor Lane

YHA

LINTON

Boss Moor

Winterburn Reservoir

Moor Lane

FLEETS

AIRTON

WINTERBURN

HETTON

RYLSTONE

Start Point

Mastiles Lane from the South

Grade: Moderate
Time: 4 Hours
Height Gain: 1414ft
Distance: 17 Miles – 12½ off road, 4½ on road
Terrain: Limestone moorland and valley
Surface: Stony, well-graded lanes, boggy bridleway, rutted drove road and busy valley roads
Start Point Grid Reference: 962591, Hetton
Maps: O.S. Yorkshire Dales 1:25 000 Southern Area

Mastiles Lane is probably the best known mountain bike route in the Yorkshire Dales. This old monastic track links Kilnsey in Wharfedale with Malham and reaches a high point of 1387ft at Holgates, a col on Kilnsey Moor. On the Kilnsey side of the col the going along Mastiles Lane is extremely good, whilst on the Malham side of the col the going can best be described as glutinous in anything but the driest weather.

On the south side of Mastiles Lane a network of bridleways and lanes criss cross Threshfield and Hetton Moors. Most of these are shooting tracks or old lanes. They are easy to follow and, when linked with Mastiles Lane, make a long but not too difficult mountain bike tour. The best link is along Smearbottoms Lane. This avoids the worst mud and ruts of Mastiles Lane and gives a fantastic 2½ mile descent into Kilnsey.

Route Description

From Hetton take Moor Lane (the bridleway at the NE end of the village) as it climbs NW for 1½m to a crossroads of bridleways and a path – ignore the bridleway on the L after ¾m. At the crossroads continue NW and descend to the ford at the head of Winterburn Reservoir. Cross the ford and join the vague bridleway on the other side. The bridleway is never very clear. It winds its way generally NW for 2m up the boggy fellside to The Weets. A trig point marks Weets Top – the actual summit of The Weets. From it descend the lane N then NW to Smearbottoms Lane.

Turn R onto Smearbottoms Lane and follow it as it works its way NE for 1½m to Mastiles Lane – the first section of Smearbottoms Lane is tarmac. Join Mastiles Lane and follow it NE over a rise then down the dip at Mastiles Gate.

Climb to the col at Holgates which is reached after 1½m. Continue NW from the col down Mastiles Lane to Kilnsey.

From Kilnsey take the B6160 S then SE for 3m to Threshfield. From Threshfield take the B6265 S for ¼m to a fork. Take the R branch and join Moor Lane. Moor Lane is then followed as it climbs W for ½m to another fork. Ignore the R branch and continue NW to the start of a bridleway. Follow the bridleway W across the moors for 1¼m to a wall and gate – the last 300yds is across heather – not on the shooting track. From the gate descend S for 1m to join Boss Moor Lane. Follow it SE for 250yds to the start of a bridleway. Join the bridleway and continue SW along the lane to the crossroads with Moor Lane passed at the beginning of the tour. At the crossroads rejoin Moor Lane and take it back down to Hetton.

Kilnsey Old Hall.

LANGSTROTHDALE CHASE AND FIRTH FELL

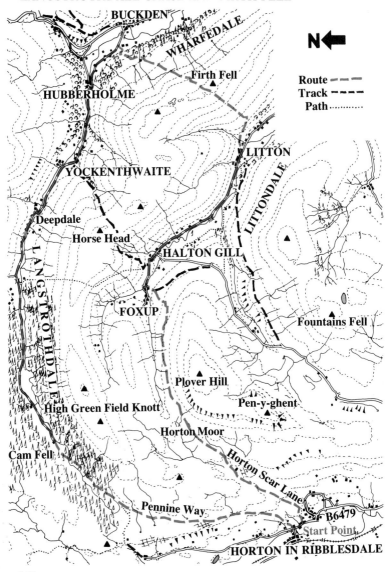

Langstrothdale Chase and Firth Fell

Grade: Very Difficult
Time: 5½ Hours
Height Gain: 2516ft
Distance: 23½ Miles – 13 off road, 10½ on road
Terrain: Valleys, high fells and exposed moorland
Surface: Steep rough lanes, boggy moorland, high pasture, roads and steep grassy bridleways.
Start Point Grid Reference: 807726, Horton in Ribblesdale
Maps: O.S. Yorkshire Dales 1:25 000 Western and Central Area, Landranger 98 1:50 000

Most obvious mountain bike routes in the Yorkshire Dales tend not to be as long or as challenging as those in the Lake District. This is due mainly to the lesser heights attained by the peaks in the Dales. To undertake a harder tour amongst the more modest peaks in the Yorkshire Dales, it is necessary to spread the net a little wider and take in tracks and bridleways which cross over a number of adjacent areas.

In the very centre of the Yorkshire Dales National Park is a circular shaped ridge of fells that separate Langstrothdale and Wharfedale from Littondale and Ribblesdale. At the eastern end of this ridge is Firth Fell which is crossed by a bridleway; whilst at the western end are two bridleways, one along Langstrothdale and one over Foxup Moor. A complete tour of these bridleways gives over 23 miles of sustained mountain biking, comparable with any to be found in the Lakes.

Route Description

Leave Horton in Ribblesdale along Horton Scar Lane which starts slightly S of, and opposite, the Penyghent Café on the B6479 (Pennine Way sign). Follow Horton Scar Lane for 1½m as it climbs a well-graded course first E then NE to Horton Moor. The lane is a popular approach route to Pen-y-ghent and, although steep and loose in parts it can be ridden along its entirety. As the gradient eases, the lane reaches a gate and junction. Three tracks leave the gate: to the R is the 'highway' up Pen-y-ghent (recently resurfaced); to the L is an access track. Take the middle course which heads NE past Hull Pot. Care should be taken when approaching Hull Pot particularly in poor visibility as the

147

track passes very close to it. Skirt round Hull Pot and continue NE along the track which steadily climbs alongside a wall. Easy but boggy riding leads to Swarth Gill Gate after 1½m.

Go through the gate and follow the track as it begins to descend across the NW flank of Plover Hill. The going becomes less boggy as a series of walls is passed. After 2m the track turns downhill (N) and starts to zigzag down towards Foxup. Follow it down for ¼m to the valley road. Take the valley road SE for 3m through Halton Gill and along Littondale to Litton.

The ascent of Firth Fell starts at Litton. It climbs the fellside behind the village to the NE. From the pub in Litton take the bridleway which climbs E up the stony lane 200yds to a fork. Continue E and take the R branch as it crosses Crystal Beck and then climbs the grassy slope to a gate. Go through the gate and follow the good track SE up the fellside. After ¼m it levels and swings in a loop round to the NE. Continue along it as it climbs directly up Firth Fell alongside the wall for ¾m to a gate. The summit trig point is 175yds SE from the gate.

From the summit of Firth Fell the bridleway continues NE and makes the long descent into Wharfedale. It crosses some steep and boggy sections but generally the going is very good and there are numerous waymarks along the route. After 2m the bridleway joins Dubbs Lane, a minor road between Buckden and Hubberholme, which is taken NW for 1m to Hubberholme. At Hubberholme join the main valley road and follow it NW for 3¾m past Yockenthwaite to a junction near Beckermonds in Langstrothdale.

At the junction near Beckermonds turn L and take the narrow road W then SW along Langstrothdale for 3m to the road's end at High Green Field. From High Green Field continue SW along the forest road for 1⅓m through the forest. Once the forest is cleared cross the ford and follow the bridleway SW for ½m to a junction on a low rise. The path R (NW) is the Pennine Way to Old Ing. Ignore this and continue SW (also the Pennine Way) then S for 3m over Birkwith Moor. Finally the superb descent along Harber Scar Lane leads back to Horton in Ribblesdale.

ADDLEBROUGH AND AYSGARTH MOOR

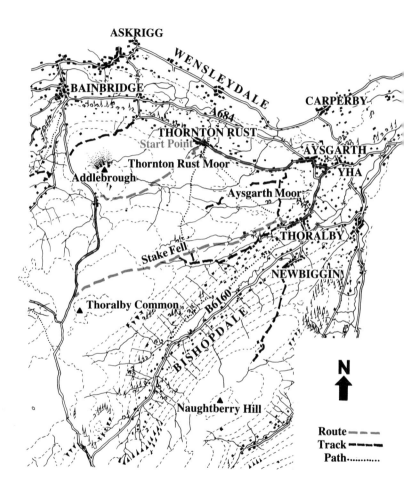

ASKRIGG

WENSLEYDALE

BAINBRIDGE

CARPERBY

A684

THORNTON RUST

Start Point

AYSGARTH

Thornton Rust Moor

YHA

Addlebrough

Aysgarth Moor

THORALBY

Stake Fell

NEWBIGGIN

B6160

Thoralby Common

BISHOPDALE

N

Naughtberry Hill

Route   - - -
Track   ━ ━ ━
Path ....

Addlebrough and Aysgarth Moor

Grade: Moderate
Time: 3 Hours
Height Gain: 1249ft
Distance: 11½ Miles – 8 off road, 3½ on road
Terrain: Open moorland and low fell
Surface: Old quarry track, boggy moorland, well-graded green lanes, hummocky moorland and roads
Start Point Grid Reference: 972888, Thornton Rust
Maps: O.S. Yorkshire Dales 1:25 000 Northern and Central Areas, O.S. Landranger 98 1:50 000

Addlebrough's stepped profile is instantly recognisable from Askrigg and Bainbridge over which it presides like a junior version of Ingleborough. Its northern slopes fall steeply into Wensleydale, whilst to the south it merges with the expansive uplands of Thornton Rust Moor and Thoralby Common, which in turn fall steeply into Bishopdale.

Traversing the southern fringe of Thoralby Common is Stake Road – a green lane which gives a continuous descent east to Thoralby of 1200 feet in 3½ miles. Except for the first ¼m, which is over grass moguls, the going is exceptional giving fast riding. To access the start of Stake Road a bridleway climbs steadily across the southern side of Addlebrough and joins Busk Lane – a pleasant walled lane which leads easily to the route's high point on Busk Moss.

Only across Thornton Rust Moor and at the start of Stake Road could navigation prove a little difficult in poor weather. This can easily be overcome with a simple compass, making this route an ideal challenge for those wanting to progress onto higher level routes.

Route Description

From the centre of Thornton Rust an old quarry track heads S. Join it and follow it to a ford. Cross the ford and take the lane straight ahead on the other side. Follow the lane as it zigzags SW up past a quarry for ½m to the start of a bridleway across pasture. The bridleway climbs steadily SW. Follow it across Thornton Rust Moor for 1½m to a broad col on the S side of Addlebrough. Head W over the col and continue along the bridleway as it winds its way down to the road at Carpley Green. Once on the road follow it S a short distance

151

through the farm to the start of Busk Lane. Busk Lane climbs steadily S. Follow it for 1m to a bend. Follow the track around the bend first W then S again for another 1m to the start of Stake Lane (bridleway sign).

Stake Lane heads NE across the moorland for ½m to a gate – the going is slow at first through the mogul-like hummocks but greatly improves past the gate. Go through the gate and follow the grassy bridleway NE for 1m to the start of a lane after a steep drop. Join the lane and continue NE along it for 2½m to a bend. This section of Stake Road is particularly fast – watch out for other users. Follow the lane R round the bend then L to a junction. Keep going straight on through the junction down into Thoralby.

From Thoralby join the road and take it N as it climbs over to Aysgarth. In Aysgarth join the A684 and follow it W through the village for 350yds to a fork. Turn L and follow the minor road W for 2m back to Thornton Rust.

Good equipment and clothing are essential.

SULBER FROM RIBBLESDALE

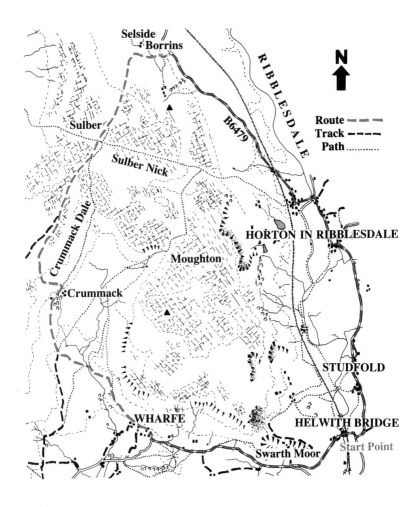

Sulber from Ribblesdale

Grade: Moderate
Time: 2 Hours
Height Gain: 600ft
Distance: 10 Miles – 4½ off road, 5½ on road
Terrain: Valley and limestone moorland
Surface: Busy valley road, narrow lanes, farm tracks and limestone pavement
Start Point Grid Reference: 810695, Helwith Bridge
Maps: O.S. Yorkshire Dales 1:25 000 Western Area, O.S. Landranger 98

The eastern side of Ingleborough is a huge tabletop expanse of limestone moorland and pavement. To the east it is bound by Ribblesdale whilst to the south it drops off in ragged fashion towards the River Wenning. Movement across this upland plateau is difficult, particularly amongst the clints and grikes of the limestone pavement. The routes that cross it tend to exploit any natural breaks. Such a route is the bridleway that crosses over Sulber; from Crummack Dale to Borrins in Ribblesdale.

The variety of the countryside along the course of this route adds particular interest to it. Down amongst the lanes of Wharfe and Crummack the going is sheltered and pleasant, whilst up on the moorland around Sulber it can feel extremely exposed especially in driving rain and mist. Once Borrins is reached a good run back can be made along the Ribblesdale road with an obligatory stop off at the excellent 'Three Peaks Café' in Horton.

Route Description

Take the Austwick road W out of Helwith Bridge for 2m to the start of a track to Wharfe – on a sharp bend. Take the track and follow it round a dog-leg to a junction by a house. Turn L and take the top fork (bridleway). Follow it through a group of houses and then continue W along it past two L turns as it then starts to climb out of Wharfe. Follow the walled lane for ¾m to a junction. Take the L fork and follow this over a ford to another junction. This is Crummack Lane. Turn R and join it, following it N to the farm at Crummack. Just to the other side of the farm, a bridleway climbs the hillside to the W. The bridleway is not too clear on the ground but it follows a course roughly parallel to the wall, gradually bending round to the N until after ¾m it breaks out onto a

155

Footbridge, Austwick Beck.

level area amongst limestone pavements where it joins a bridleway from Clapham.

From the junction the bridleway heads NE across the open expanses of Thieves Moss and Sulber. Mostly the going is fast over smooth grass although there is the odd section of limestone pavement to catch out the unwary. Follow the bridleway for 2m to join the B6479 at Borrins. The first section is level and passes through Sulber Gate and then starts to descend through pasture. Through the pasture the course of the bridleway is vague: it finally swings E at a ford on the S side of the farm at Borrins. Once on the B6479 it is simply a matter of turning R and following it for 4m back to Helwith Bridge passing through Horton in Ribblesdale en route.

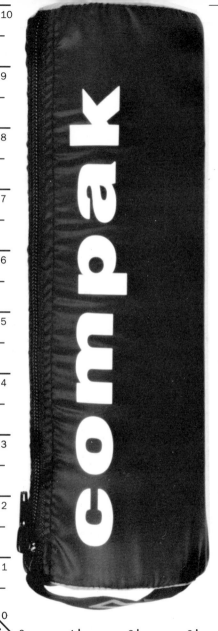

MOUNTAIN BIKER

THE MAGAZINE WITH ITS FINGER ON THE PULSE AND ITS FEET ON THE PEDALS

READ IT EVERY MONTH FOR THE BEST TOURS, TRAINING, RACES REPORTS AND TECHNICAL FEATURES

100 PAGES FOR ONLY £1.95

MOUNTAIN

BIKER

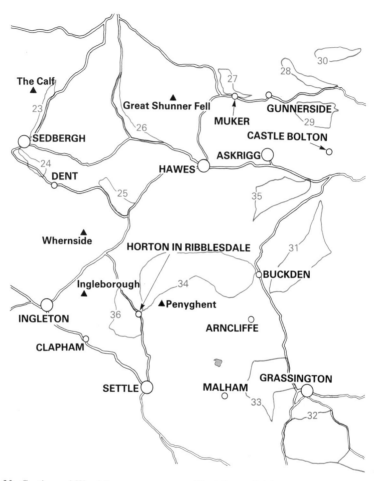